The Lawyer's
Winning Edge

EXCEPTIONAL COURTROOM PERFORMANCE

"Matheo and DeCaro's book does a novel job of "tell and show" where many other books fall short. *The Lawyer's Winning Edge* is full of practical advice for attorneys supported by terrific techniques that they both describe and show through the accompanying CD. If you want to put your best foot forward in courtroom delivery, read this book.

—Dr. Karen Lisko, Ph.D.,
Senior Litigation Consultant,
Holland & Hart

"This book is clear, wise, funny, eloquent, and eminently useful. Do you need more? Like Len and Lisa in person, it does not magnify itself beyond what it can absolutely deliver: enriched understanding and ability to communicate more effectively in calling your audience to action."

—Joshua Karton

"This is a great how-to-do-it book for trial lawyers. While experienced trial lawyers can more easily implement their teachings, anyone who wants to communicate effectively with jurors should read it—more than once!

—K. Preston Oade, Jr.,
Holme, Roberts and Owen

HOW BRADFORD PUBLISHING HELPS YOU HELP YOUR CLIENTS

Founded in 1881, Bradford Publishing Company is Colorado's oldest and most trusted publisher of legal forms, law books, and legal information. Bradford Publishing upholds high standards of quality that are applied to all of its products. We monitor legislation, court rule changes, and agency regulations to assure that our publications are current and accurate. Colorado attorneys rely on our printed and electronic forms to save them the time and expense of drafting forms from scratch—knowing that all our forms are accepted by Colorado courts.

Although Bradford Publishing specializes in Colorado products, many of our publications, like *The Lawyer's Winning Edge*, are not state-specific and are **helpful tools for attorneys everywhere**.

Other books that can help you in your practice are:

Law of the Web: A Field Guide to Internet Publishing

Any attorney working with a client who has a web site can benefit from this book. As Internet usage has mushroomed, a body of law has begun to take shape to govern this new frontier. Author/expert Jonathan Hart, of the prestigious Washington, D.C. law firm Dow, Lohnes and Albertson, has done the research for you. With the author's helpful analysis and insightful commentary, this book tracks the important legal developments—court cases and legislation—that are now impacting anyone who is providing information via the Internet. *Law of the Web* also addresses key issues that are likely to become significant to Internet users in the future.

This book, with real-life case-by-case examples of people who were rewarded by doing it right and those who got busted for doing it wrong, will help you protect your clients.

Collaborative Law: A New Model for Dispute Resolution

Intended for litigation attorneys, especially in family law, employment law, worker's comp, and other intensely emotional areas of law. Professionals in litigation support fields, such as mediators, accountants, mental health professionals, child advocates, and other experts will also find *Collaborative Law* useful. This book includes an overview of collaborative law; discussion of the skills, knowledge and attitude required of the participants; components of a "multi-disciplinary" collaborative team; steps in the collaborative process; starting a collaborative law practice; ethical issues, including malpractice concerns, duties, and confidentiality; case processing and coordination with the courts; and selected forms.

How to Find Us

We invite you to visit us in any of the following ways:
- Retail store in downtown Denver, Colorado at 1743 Wazee Street
- Customer Service and mail order—(303) 292-2590 or (800) 446-2831
- Our web site at www.bradfordpublishing.com

www.bradfordpublishing.com

The Lawyer's
Winning Edge

EXCEPTIONAL COURTROOM PERFORMANCE

By
Lisa L. DeCaro & Leonard Matheo

With a Foreword by
James W. McElhaney

BRADFORD PUBLISHING COMPANY
Denver, Colorado

Disclaimer

This book is intended to provide general information with regard to the subject matter covered. It is not meant to provide legal opinions or to offer advice, nor to serve as a substitute for advice by licensed, legal or other professionals. This book is sold with the understanding that Bradford Publishing Company and the authors, by virtue of its publication, are not engaged in rendering legal or other professional services to the reader.

Bradford Publishing Company and the authors do not warrant that the information contained in this book is complete or accurate, and do not assume and hereby disclaim any liability to any person for any loss or damage caused by errors, inaccuracies or omissions, or usage of this book.

Laws, and interpretations of those laws, change frequently, and the subject matter of this book can have important legal consequences that may vary from one individual to the next. It is therefore the responsibility of the reader to know whether, and to what extent, this information is applicable to his or her situation, and if necessary, to consult legal, tax, or other counsel.

Library of Congress Cataloging-in-Publication Data

DeCaro, Lisa L.
  The lawyer's winning edge : exceptional courtroom performance / by Lisa L. Decaro and Leonard Matheo.
     p. cm.
  ISBN 1-883726-92-1
  1. Trial practice--United States. I. Matheo, Leonard. II. Title.

  KF8915.D42 2004
  347.73'504--dc22

                                        2003028047

Cover design by Cynthia Fonseca
The Lawyer's Winning Edge—Exceptional Courtroom Performance
ISBN: 1-883726-92-1

Published 2004 by Bradford Publishing Company
1743 Wazee Street, Denver, Colorado 80202
www.bradfordpublishing.com

Contents

About The Authors

Leonard Matheo and **Lisa L. DeCaro** are the founders of Courtroom Performance, Inc. (CPI), a trial consulting firm dedicated to improving oral advocacy and the visual presentation of evidence. Professional actors and directors, each has over 15 years of experience in professional theater, film, and television. Ms. DeCaro and Mr. Matheo have helped thousands of attorneys and their witnesses prepare for deposition and trial, by employing the professional actor's techniques of effective story analysis, story structure, and persuasive presentation.

Ms. DeCaro and Mr. Matheo are active members of the American Society of Trial Consultants and the Association for Continuing Legal Education. Both are frequent speakers at regional seminars and national conventions (including the annual conference of the ABA Litigation Leadership Section and many state bar programs), and have served as faculty for colleges and conferences nationwide (including UCLA Law School and the University of Colorado School of Law). Ms. DeCaro and Mr. Matheo have also authored popular papers and articles for national legal publications (including ALI-ABA's *Practical Litigator,* ABA's *Tips from the Trenches,* and *The Brief.*)

CPI utilizes a practical system of presentation techniques as they apply to the courtroom, to help trial attorneys enhance their ability to advocate for their clients. Through seminars, workshops, publications, and trial consulting, CPI helps litigators compose a compelling opening statement and closing argument, explain how to use non-verbal communication and eye contact to emphasize their message, how to build a relationship with each juror, how to call the jurors to action, and how to advance their story through each phase of the trial.

To learn more about Lisa DeCaro, Len Matheo, CPI, and the services they offer, visit their website at www.courtroomperformance.com, or contact them by calling (800) 818-6755.

Foreword

They ought to cover this book with old oak barrel staves and bind it with black iron straps, because it's a treasure chest—and the gems inside are real.

Not cute little trial tricks. Not deceptive new ploys to conceal old frauds. Not clever bits of misdirection, phony theatricality, or contrived dramatic moments.

If that's what you want, put it down. This book is not what the "Spin Doctor" ordered.

Instead, it's filled with genuine insights, ideas, and techniques that work. And a whole new way for how to look at yourself and your role as a courtroom communicator.

Take "Killing Lawyer Man" for example. Lisa DeCaro and Len Matheo show you how to free yourself from that pretentious veneer you started putting on the day you entered law school. They teach you how to develop the habits of voice inflection, emphasis, and eye contact used by professional speakers (after all, speaking is one of the most important things you do for a living). They help you become natural and unaffected in front of others. Best of all, they start you step by step down the road to becoming a captivating storyteller.

Go ahead. Turn to any page and read the first thing that catches your eye. What you will find will be: Simple. Honest. Disarming. Occasionally Counter-Intuitive and Always Effective.

The Lawyer's Winning Edge is one of the most remarkable books for trial lawyers I've ever seen. With the exercises and demonstrations on the video CD-ROM that comes with the book, Len and Lisa show you how to do what they're talking about. This is a whole course on how to develop the presentational skills you need to teach the judge and jury the facts that will win your case.

— James W. McElhaney
February 2004

Preface

"Who's stupid, crazy idea was this?" we said to each other as we were rehearsing our first workshop for attorneys. Prior to this statement, we had spent many months preparing to teach the skills that professional actors use in order to be persuasive and engaging in front of an audience. Lisa's father, an attorney from a family of attorneys, had suggested that we use our expertise to help trial lawyers do a better job for their clients. At first we balked. Why would lawyers listen to a couple of actors with no law degree? Finally, having been inspired by our friend and mentor, Joshua Karton, and after many months of research, we felt we were ready. That is, until we began our "dress rehearsal" the night before that first workshop.

After about two hours of rehearsal we were finished. We had run out of brilliant nuggets! Our program the next day was scheduled for a full eight hours. We were about to get up in front of a group of lawyers and try to teach them how to be better advocates in the courtroom. What in the world had we gotten ourselves in to?

"Who's stupid, crazy idea was this?"

After much anxious discussion, we made a pivotal decision—a decision that has served us well in all that we do. We made a conscious decision to stick to what we know. We vowed not to be led into a discussion about information that was outside our expertise.

It all worked out surprisingly well. We ended up speaking for longer than our scheduled eight hours, talking through lunch and all of the breaks. The people who had paid to hear us didn't want to see another lawyer giving a CLE workshop. They wanted a different perspective, and they wanted to gain an edge in the courtroom over their opponents. And of course, they did not want us to talk about areas in which we had no experience. Instead, we talked about our years in the theater and the skills and techniques that great actors use to captivate an audience, and how an attorney can use these skills persuade a judge and jury.

Now, after teaching thousands of attorneys these skills, after consulting with hundreds of lawyers on hundreds of different cases, and after watching hundreds of jurors deliberate in mock trials, we felt that it was time to share our thoughts and experience, and teach the skills and techniques that have made all of the lawyers we have worked with much more effective advocates.

A lawyer who is a successful advocate in the courtroom is skilled with oral argument and knows that an effective argument must be informative, conversational, and relaxed, yet passionate, authoritative and compelling—all at the same time. *The Lawyer's Winning Edge: Exceptional Courtroom Performance* provides practical tips and persuasive techniques that will help give you the winning edge in the courtroom.

You will learn how to create a captivating opening statement and a powerful closing argument, as well as how to use nonverbal communication and eye contact to emphasize your message. This book will show you how to build a relationship with each juror, how to call the jurors to action, and how to advance your story through each phase of the trial.

The book also includes a valuable *video* CD-ROM[1], playable on your computer's CD-ROM drive, that demonstrates breathing, vocal skills and inflection, body language, gestures, and eye contact exercises. These exercises will help you perfect your communication skills and make your most dynamic and convincing case ever.

This book is not about giving you tips and tricks in order to "fool your audience" into agreeing with your position, or to "put one over" on the jury. In our years of working with lawyers and watching hundreds of jurors deliberate in mock trials and jury research, there is one thing of which we are confident: Jurors—in this day and age of television and sound bytes—have highly sensitive and refined "lie detectors." These lie detectors are hard-wired in all of us. Open and honest communication between an attorney and the judge and jury is the highest goal. Persuasive communication requires honesty, credibility, and a sincere connection with your audience. It requires listening. And it is extremely exciting to watch.

Simply put, this book is about the communication process at work between human beings and the tools and skills needed to persuade in a legal setting. This book also carries with it an

---

[1] The video CD-ROM is attached to the inside of the back cover of this book. You must have a sound card and speakers connected to your computer in order to hear the audio portion of the CD-ROM.

added bonus: the skills and techniques that you learn here are applicable in your day-to-day life as well as in front of a judge, jury, master, or arbitration panel. For in the end, it all comes down to a conversation. A conversation with one or with many, with replies or without. You may find that you are re-learning many one-on-one communication skills that you may have once known. We hope that this book will heighten your awareness of how you talk, listen and learn on a daily basis.

— Lisa DeCaro and Len Matheo
February 2004

Acknowledgements

This has been the hardest part of this book to write. Since we view this book as the culmination of the experience we've accumulated in the years since we founded Courtroom Performance, Inc., we feel we must show our sincere gratitude not only to the people who helped get this book off the ground, but also to the people who helped us start—and continue—our firm.

Our deep, heartfelt thanks go to many such people:

First, to our family: Phil DeCaro, Gale Gatto, Bob and Pauline Matheo, Tony Matheo, Barbara DeCaro, Jeffrey DeCaro, Lara DeCaro, and Phillip G. DeCaro. They provided free legal services, free editorial services, free marketing services, free tax services, and financial support to pay for the things we needed that weren't free. Your encouragement, love, and support—of all kinds—made this very improbable venture possible.

To the people at Bradford Publishing who made this book a reality. To Greg Smith, who made sure we actually finished the book, instead of just thinking about it. To Reda Martin, who didn't hesitate when Greg said, "Hey, I think we should do this book." To Peter Klann and Brent Beltrone, whose marketing expertise probably contributed to your buying this book. To Marsi Buckmelter, who made us look good with her editing skills. To Lisa Travis Fischer, who kept us on track, and kept us calm in the face of a few somewhat scary deadlines. To Karen

Remley, who organized and coordinated our CD-ROM, telling us that we looked great exactly when we most needed to hear it. And to Leslie Myers, David Kroll, Paul Burks, and everyone at the State Bar of Texas, for providing the beautiful facilities, exceptional skills, and wonderful advice that made the CD-ROM a reality.

To our dear friend and mentor Joshua Karton, a pioneer in this field, who could have told us, "Good luck, kids," but instead told us, "Please just let me know how I can help you." You are a true teacher. Your willingness to share your immense talent and expertise with us has touched our lives, and our hearts.

To one of the greatest storytellers, trial lawyers, and teachers we've had the fortune to meet, James McElhaney, whose books inspired us even before we considered him a friend.

To Gary Abrams of Colorado Bar Association CLE, who thought we might be crazy when we first met, but hired us anyway. To Mark Carroll of ALI-ABA, the very first to believe that we really could write a whole book. To Dr. Karen Lisko, Dr. Shelley Spiecker, and Richard Gabriel, whose generosity and integrity have helped improve the entire consulting field. To Steve Rosen, and Graham and Anna Marie Thatcher, who set the bar so high for entertaining education with their CLE programs.

To Mark Kennedy, Mal Wheeler, Jack Trigg, and the rest of the firm of Wheeler, Trigg & Kennedy, for showing us what can be accomplished by talented trial lawyers who believe in what we teach. To Maria Collier, for all of her enthusiasm and encouragement, both personally and professionally. To every-one at Jenkens & Gilchrist, P.C., for inspiring us with their dedication to continuous improvement. To Carolyn Cockrell, who was one of the first to take a chance on these "actor types," and who did it with unshakeable confidence. To Alan Cotler, who helped to reinvigorate our program. And to Preston Oade, who showed us that some trial lawyers still do believe in magic—and that these are the great ones.

And finally, to these and all of the lawyers we have had the privilege of working with over the years. We learn as much from you as you learn from us.

Introduction

Killing *Lawyer Man*

We were teaching a seminar in Richmond, Virginia, and we asked the participants to tell us what made them choose to attend our program. Most said things like, "I want to learn how to deal with stage fright," or "I want to learn what to do with my hands," or "I want to know how to tell a better story."

One very tall man stood up and said, in his deep Southern drawl, "I want to kill *Lawyer Man*."

We blinked. The class looked frightened. He explained:

> "If I tell you about my case over dinner, I am passionate and concise. I talk like a real person, and I'm really persuasive. But when I stand up in the courtroom to tell a jury about my case, I become *Lawyer Man*. That man who isn't me in the courtroom. That persona and face that I put on in front of the jury. *Lawyer Man* is the picture in my head of what a good lawyer looks like, but that picture is nothing like me. I don't know who it is, to tell you the truth, but it ain't me, that's for sure!"

Lawyer Man is a good description of what happens to so many attorneys—male and female—when they stand up in the courtroom. Suddenly, passionate advocates sound stilted or awkward, melodramatic or monotonous, pretentious or unconfident, frenetic or boring.

And why shouldn't this happen? Attorneys—even trial attorneys—are not taught how to be great speakers. Very rarely do most attorneys actually get into the courtroom. We put trial lawyers into an extremely stressful situation, with a tremendous amount at stake, and ask them to do something that most Americans fear more than being buried alive: speak in public. And they're not just being asked to speak in public. They also have to write the script, direct the show, and prepare all of the other actors in the drama. Why would we expect them to miraculously, spontaneously, become great speakers?

What's the key?

There's an old story about two Greek orators: Pericles and Demosthenes. At different times during Greece's history, the country was at war, and powerful speeches were made to rally the people behind the effort. Pericles was known as a great speaker, and when his time came, he used that talent to inspire the public. When he finished speaking the people applauded. They said, "What a great speech!"

Demosthenes, on the other hand, was not known as a great speaker. In fact, legend has it that he overcame a speech impediment forcing himself to speak with pebbles in his mouth. But Demosthenes was a man of the people, and he felt passionate about their cause. When he finished speaking, the people said, "Let's march!"

Pericles was a good platform speaker. Nowadays, we'd call him a keynote speaker. Demosthenes was a persuasive speaker. He'd make a great trial lawyer.

One question we're frequently asked is, "What's the key to being a great storyteller?" As Demosthenes proved, you don't need to be a "perfect" speaker. You don't need to be tall or handsome or beautiful. You don't need to be brilliant. You don't need to be born with that illusive "it" that some movie stars have.

To be a persuasive speaker, you need to be credible. You need to be able to build—and maintain—the trust of the audience. To do that, you need to make the audience feel comfortable and confident in your ability, and—as Demosthenes did—in your passionate conviction in your cause. Engendering this feeling in the audience is a skill. It is a skill that *Lawyer Man* does not have, but that every one of you can learn and master. You need to be able to appear confident and certain—even when you're not. You need to be able to use your voice in a way that keeps the attention of your audience, and you need to be able to control your voice for an extended period of time. You need to be able to modify the inflection of your voice to express the meaning behind your words. You need to be able to use body language that enhances your argument. You need to be able to use eye contact to build a strong relationship with each person in your "audience." You need to be able to structure your story in a way that is clear and engaging to the trier of fact. You need to be able to communicate a passionate belief in your cause, even if you don't feel it today. And, to keep them listening for an extended period of time, you need to have a certain amount of "stage presence."

All of these things are physical and mental skills that can be learned and practiced. And the goal of all of it is to build credibility—to kill *Lawyer Man*. It seems odd that people spend so many years learning skills to help them appear more "natural" on stage, but that is precisely what it takes. Public speaking is not a "natural" occurrence. You would never use the eye contact techniques in this book when you are talking to your family around the dinner table. Public speaking—particularly when the goal is persuasion—requires that you be conversational yet presentational.

Great stage actors spend years in school (and/or "on the boards") learning this, because they know that great theater is born from honest, credible, and believable communication. In truth, great acting doesn't look—or feel—like acting at all. We use the word "feel" because in this book we will be teaching you the skills of communication that go beyond just the words that come out of your mouth. The *art* is communication: connecting with your audience on a deep, personal level, and connecting at the core level, one human being at a time.

It all comes down to this: the key to being a great storyteller is first being comfortable (or at least *appearing* comfortable) being yourself in front of a group of people. You are far more persuasive than *Lawyer Man*. If you practice the skills discussed in this book, you will master feeling comfortable in front of people. Afterwards, you are free to add the icing on the cake: the storytelling skills that will take you to the next level of persuasive communication.

Perception versus reality

Many people talk about making a "good first impression." Obviously, that's a goal with any encounter in which there is something valuable at stake. Job interviews, first dates, client meetings, public speeches, and, of course, the courtroom.

First impressions are definitely important. However, first impressions are not immutable. They can be changed—but why have that issue to overcome?

First impressions are very complicated. When you meet someone new, the impression you get from that person is influenced by your past experiences, your preconceptions, your value system. The person you are meeting can only control a portion of the impression you develop of him or her. So it is with you in the courtroom. You can dress right, look right, and talk right. This is a great start, but you're also dealing with the past experiences, preconceptions, and value system of each juror. One of them may have a shaky first impression of you because you look a bit like his obnoxious Uncle Frank. You can do your best, but you can't control every aspect of your first impression.

What you can control is yourself. You can make sure that you do nothing to interfere with your message. You can control the picture you paint for the jurors. You can control your body language, to make sure that you are not doing something to contradict your argument. You can control the tone and quality of your voice. You can control the structure of your story— the perspective you use, the tense, the emphasis.

The intent of this book is to help you learn compelling and persuasive oral advocacy. Public speaking is a physical and mental skill set, like driving a car or playing tennis. Add to that skill set good writing and good story structure, and you have compelling and persuasive oral advocacy.

This book is a training manual, to guide you in the art of speaking and communicating. In this book, we share some of our stories of how we've applied our theater skills to life in the courtroom. This book is not intended as a self-help book, and we hope that none of it reads like pop psychology. The truth of the matter is that in order to be an excellent communicator, both in private and in public, you must be comfortable with yourself. All emotions, such as fear or apprehension, are allowed in the arena of public communications. But most importantly, to overcome our fears and apprehensions, we must be courageous enough to show them to the world. Thus do we become persuasive and compelling.

So, we'd like you to keep in mind the following bits of advice when reading this book.

- Don't just read it once. Read it once, and then read it again, practicing what you learn. By reading it more than once, you'll gain fresh insights.

- View and review the enclosed CD-ROM. It will provide examples of the physical skills we discuss in Parts 1 and 3 of the book.

- Keep an open mind. We heard it once said that when you hear a speaker or read a new book you should "be open and aware of what you initially disagree with." For nothing is learned when we agree absolutely with the communicator. Many times, it just makes us feel good about ourselves, and "right." When we disagree, that's where the gold is. That's where the possibility for change and growth exists. Unlike most books in the legal profession, this book is going to challenge you to re-think a concept or way of doing things. To really understand some of the concepts of communication, you may find some of your basic beliefs about yourself challenged. Usually, this is where those "ah-ha!" moments lie.

Actors and advocates

Actors and trial attorneys, in fact, have little in common as a profession. While attorneys are diligently constructing their case, gathering evidence, creating briefs and filing motions, negotiating with and confronting the other side, actors are probably gathered in the classroom playing "theater games" to hone their capacity for spontaneity and creativity. They are developing the tools they will need to perform, such as their voice, their body, and their ability to analyze the words of the author and translate them into a physical action. After school they may be out hitting the pavement looking for work, or if they are working as an actor and not performing some interim job, perhaps they are rehearsing a script or trying out different ways of approaching a character they're playing.

> **Fact:** Ninety-eight percent of actors who belong to one of the working unions (SAG, AFTRA, AEA) are not working. They spend the majority of their time either looking for work or working an interim job until they can find work as an actor. Now aren't you glad you went to law school instead?

So what can you, the advocate, learn from the actor? Actors spend many hours preparing for performance. In school, they learn skills that enable them to control their presence on the stage, skills as simple as how to stand still and be interesting. They learn how to use their voice dramatically in order to have the most impact on their audience. They learn through trial and error which gestures work and which do not. They learn how to express their own "stage presence," which opens new doorways to communicating with an audience. All of these skills can be learned, practiced, and perfected. Although some of us may naturally possess more of these skills than others, they all can be learned. Just as in a magic show, the magic one creates with an audience isn't really magical at all. Anyone can do it.

Great actors are masters in *orally* communicating the meaning embedded in the *written* word. Take Shakespeare, for example. For many a juror, a trial lawyer's opening statement can be like hearing Shakespeare done badly in the theater. Jurors know that the lawyer is saying something interesting and important; they just don't know what. When a trial lawyer has his or her opening statement outlined and then begins to speak it aloud, suddenly the message changes in a deep and fundamental way. It's not written communication anymore. Now it is oral communication, and it needs to be treated that way or else it will not be understood.

A great actor is also a master in using the body as an instrument of communication. Obviously, *what you say* in the courtroom is vital. But communication is more than just the words that come out of your mouth. In the courtroom, the jury is looking at how you communicate as a whole person. What does your body language say to the jury? Is it contradicting your argument? Is it enhancing what you say? The great actor speaks as a whole person—again, the way that we communicate honestly in the real world.

A great actor has been trained in the *art* of communication. The lawyer, primarily, has not. For the most part, the only way the lawyer learns this art is by trial and error, and by watching others do it (often badly). This book, however, is just the beginning. After going through this book and the interactive exercises on the enclosed CD-ROM, you will be well on your way to being a master communicator. You will also see a major difference in your presentation effectiveness. But in order to be a master, you will need to practice and practice and practice with an ongoing level of commitment.

The goals of this book

In this book, we teach you the skills of acting that apply to your life in the courtroom. Whether you are arguing in front of a judge or jury, or in deposition or voir dire, or whether you are making a presentation to your friends or colleagues, these skills will make you become more present, interesting, and most importantly, a more effective communicator.

It's important to mention here that this is not an "acting book" for attorneys. We have painstakingly researched the needs of attorneys in and out of the courtroom. We have helped many lawyers prepare their cases. We have helped them prepare key witnesses, as well as opening statements and closing arguments. This book reflects that experience, as well as our experience on stage and film. We've taken the skills that actors and directors use—to convey a story, control a stage, and persuade an audience—and applied them to the needs of the busy trial attorney.

This book provides the skills that attorneys need to construct a persuasive argument and confidently tell a compelling story.

The foundation

We begin with the foundation of great public speaking: the physical skills that make you appear confident and focused, and allow you to connect with the trier of fact.

Remember, you are learning physical skills. You are creating new habits. New habits require practice. The next time you stand up in court, you don't want to start thinking, "I should be standing like this," or "I should be using this technique to make eye contact." You want to be free to focus on your *message,* and on your listeners. To be a good driver, you can't think consciously about every single movement in the series of movements necessary to operate your car. For this reason, each section of this book contains practice exercises to help you learn your new skills so they become new habits that you can rely on when the adrenaline starts flowing.

The icing on the cake

After you've mastered these foundations, you're able to effectively add the icing on the cake: the storytelling skills discussed in the latter part of this book. When you tell a story—when you tell a jury what happened—each individual sees a picture in his or her head. These story techniques are designed to help you take control of that picture. If the trier of fact looks at the facts and sees the same thing that you see, then you can lead her to the ending you see.

Becoming "other-focused"

One theme recurs throughout this book, and that is to take your focus off yourself and put it on your listeners. Become the most *interested* person in the courtroom, not the most *interesting*.

Most of the presentation mistakes novices make are the result of self-consciousness. If you are self-conscious, you will feel—and look—uncomfortable, unconfident, and unfocused. Remember, when you stand up in the courtroom, it isn't about you. It isn't about how good you look, or even what a great speaker you are. It's about your message. As with Demosthenes, it's about calling your audience to action.

So, even though this book would *appear* to be about you, the advocate, it is actually about the *listener* receiving your message. It is about doing everything you can to make it easier for the listener to see your picture, accept your message, agree with your themes, and deliver your verdict.

Your comfort level

Now that we've discussed the importance of being—or at least appearing to be—comfortable with yourself in front of a group of people, we should define what we mean by "comfortable." Tension is normal in any communication where there is something at stake. We do not mean that you must—or even should—eliminate those butterflies that you feel before a presentation. The skills we share in this book are designed to make you *look* confident and credible. Eventually, these skills become second nature and you feel more confident.

Further, when you learn new skills, it is rarely comfortable at first. Sometimes when we work with a client and his physical presentation becomes more *effective*, it doesn't feel *comfortable* to him at first. That's when we break the news: we don't care. When it comes right down to it, courtroom advocacy isn't about your comfort; it's about your message. So, if you are more comfortable talking in a low volume, which makes it too hard on the trier of fact, then you have to practice increasing your volume until you become comfortable talking at a more effective volume. Obviously, we'd like you to be comfortable up there. But it's even more important for you to be effective, and look comfortable.

Actors know that if they are uncomfortable, it probably means they are finding and trying new things. Stretching yourself is the best way to grow. If you've bought this book, you probably know that.

A final word

It comes down to this: you're more persuasive as yourself. And you are most persuasive when you are simply being yourself, focused on your listeners. Doing that is a physical skill, which can be learned and practiced.

So take the leap, and kill *Lawyer Man.* Or at least wound him a bit.

Part 1.

The Foundation For Communication

There are just three essentials to a good story: humanity, a point, and the storyteller."

— J. Frank Dobie

"You don't have to be right. All you have to do is be candid."

— Allen Ginsberg

"Leap, and the net will appear."

— Julia Cameron

Chapter 1:
"The key is sincerity, and once you learn to fake that, you've got it made!" ... And Other Really Bad Advice

Why are there so many people out there telling so many other people the wrong things about public speaking? There are many giving advice, but no one addresses the main issue: how we communicate one-on-one and how we communicate with a group of people, what's the same and what's different, and how we direct focus to our message.

In life, so much of our day-to-day communication is overwhelmed with facades, and most of what we are communicating relates to image. Usually, these images we project are quite simple: strength, anger, concern, happiness, love, kindness, confidence, and so on.

And herein lies the problem with what most people these days are passing off as public speaking training. Most teachers and trainers try to teach us how to "show" the emotions mentioned above. Hence, they may tell the student to smile when they give a speech because studies show that an audience is more receptive to a friendly face. Or they may tell the student to look people in the eye, because that will communicate honesty or trust. The problem, however, is that in telling people to be happy, or to be confident or to be concerned, we have effectively told them to "act" or "pretend" when they are speaking. The result is dishonest, phony communication.

When we attempt to teach people how to project a certain image, we set ourselves up for dishonest communication. Haven't we all seen the salesperson whom we just don't trust, or have been aroused by a public speaker, but then we become suspicious when he tries to sell us his latest book at the end of the presentation? So how do we teach the art of effective communication? How do we honestly—and with integrity—communicate passion, concern, authority, credibility, or righteous indignation? First, let's define what we mean buy "effective communication."

Why do we communicate in the first place? Usually, it is to get a specific result from another person or group. Actors call it "playing an intention" or "playing an objective." In other words, I want you to do something in response to what I am saying. It is my intention to make you do something. For instance, when we enter a fast-food restaurant and order a sandwich, we are asking the person behind the counter for a specific sandwich. We attempt to use the most effective words. We want the sandwich, and we are "playing that objective" to cause the other person to give us a sandwich. We try, though not always successfully, to communicate effectively to reach that goal. Have you ever tried to special order something in a restaurant and you find yourself tongue-tied, trying to explain to the server exactly what it is you want?

Whether ordering a sandwich or trying to persuade a judge or jury that your cause is the right one, the first step is still the same: to define your intention (what you want the listener to actively do in response to your communication). Making your motives conscious and intentional is the first step in the process.

Next, you want to find out what the listener's needs are regarding what you want. Are they compatible? Are they able to hear, understand, and believe in your message the way you are communicating it?

Finally, and most importantly, focus your attention and actions on helping the listeners obtain what they need to make the decisions you need them to make. The mindset of your communication is the most important element.

Let's say, for example, that you are defending ACME Tool Company in a product liability suit. You want to communicate your theory of the case, which is that the tool was being used irresponsibly and that there is nothing wrong with the product. You have accomplished the first step by knowing what exactly it is that *you want* to communicate.

Now, here is where the plot thickens. Most attorneys never move beyond that first step ("What do I want to say?"). But the next step has little to do with what you want. The next step is all about the trier of fact. What do members of a jury need to help them understand and see the case clearly? Do they need to know about the painstaking research and design that went into this product? Probably. Do they need to know what the plaintiff was doing the night before the accident? Quite possibly. Do they need five different experts to tell them the same thing: that most accidents are due to human error? Maybe not. What specific details do the jurors need to know in order to understand your point of view?

And finally, you need to focus your attention and intention on helping them see your picture and come to the same conclusions that you did. Your focus is on specifically communicating the information they need to help them make a decision, and not on helping them see a simple image of you, such as "confident," "authoritative," "angry that your client is being accused," and so on.

More bad advice ... and by the way, all of these stories are true!

A woman in the back raised her hand. The public speaking "expert" acknowledged her, "Yes, you have a question?" The woman stood (she was about five feet tall), and said, "I feel so self-conscious when I stand up in front of a group. I never know what to do with my hands!" She laughed nervously, and sat back down as quickly as possible. The "expert" said, "Oh, that's not a problem. Just put them on the sides of the lectern."

This is a true story. And that poor woman had paid good money for this?

Gestures and body language are an important part of your arsenal when it comes to persuasion. Why eliminate your ability to use them—and thus reduce your effectiveness—just because you feel uncomfortable and don't know what to do with your hands? Speaking is a physical skill and can be learned. There are specific exercises and advice regarding body language in Chapter 4.

And still more

John was an excellent attorney. He was a good speaker, too. He structured an exciting argument. He modulated his tone of voice, inflection, and volume to illustrate important points and keep the jurors engaged. His one big problem was that he had a hard time "connecting" with the jurors. He could put on a great show, but he couldn't go deeper. He was having a problem making effective eye contact—his eyes just didn't seem to be making real contact. When we tried to work with him on this, he got a bit nervous and said, "I was told that since some people don't like eye contact, I shouldn't look them right in the eye. I was told I should actually look at their forehead, instead."

Terrible, and dangerous, advice. Here's an acting tip: One of the skills an actor will employ to play a blind person on stage is by looking at the forehead of the other actors on stage. This way, they are doing what a blind person does: looking in the right general direction, but not making a connection. Eye contact in our society is extremely important. In a courtroom, it is vital, not just because people don't trust someone who can't look them in the eye, but also because if you are not making effective eye contact with your jurors then you can not possibly be "listening" to them. You can't possibly be the most interested person in the courtroom if you aren't making that connection. (We discuss eye contact techniques in detail in Chapter 5.)

Beware

People mean well; they offer you advice to be helpful. However, some people have a hard time expressing what they think you should do in language that is both clear and constructive. Some advice is not helpful, some makes you more self-conscious, and some is just plain wrong. The point is: question the advice you receive about public speaking.

Remember these four important truths, and filter all advice through them:

1. **Every speaker is different.** There is no "right" presentation style. What is perfect for me may be awful for you. Be honest with yourself, and with your audience, at all times.

2. **Never try to "be" anything.** If you try to "be authoritative," you'll end up looking arrogant. If you try to "be confident," you'll end up looking awkward. Instead of trying to "be" something, try to "do" things that accomplish your goals. If you want to appear confident, do what confident people do: stand up tall, with your feet approximately shoulders' width apart. Balance your weight. Come out from behind the lectern or table. Make effective eye contact. Allow gestures to convey the meaning of your words. Speak strongly, with enough volume to be heard easily at the back of the room. Pause for emphasis. Smile when appropriate.

3. **Your focus should always be on your audience.** Self-consciousness is just that: being overly conscious of

yourself. Become conscious of your audience—their needs, their reactions, their mannerisms, their habits, their values. Everything you do should make it easier for them to listen, to understand, to argue your case in deliberations, to teach their spouse everything they've learned about how a new product is tested.

4. **Your biggest asset is your credibility.** Never, under any circumstances, do *anything* that will diminish your credibility. You may have the most brilliant argument since the Gettysburg Address, but it won't mean anything if the jurors simply don't believe you.

Any advice that you receive should work within these four filters. If someone you trust is trying to help and their advice is not clear, ask them to be specific about what you are *doing* that they think is ineffective. If an expert tells you to do something that clearly puts *your* comfort ahead of your audience, then think carefully about whether that is truly good advice. As we discussed earlier, something that instantly feels comfortable may not be the most effective: indeed, many elements of effective communication feel uncomfortable until you've gotten used to them. Beware of shortcuts.

Sometimes, bad advice just needs to be translated into an action—something you can do, which makes it easier for your listener, and boosts your credibility.

Give serious thought to all advice and try to figure out what the person giving the advice is responding to. You can't necessarily "trust your instincts" about whether it is good advice or bad. Anything new will feel uncomfortable at first, and as we said earlier, your comfort is less important than your audience's understanding of your message.

Read, learn, practice, and then practice some more. That's the best way to learn how to handle advice—the good, the bad, and the ugly.

Chapter 2:
How To Use Your Voice To Create
"Vocal Thunder" In The Courtroom

Try this exercise: Take a deep breath and hold it in. How does it feel? Do you feel tension in your chest, your throat, your face? Now try to speak the first sentence of your opening statement. How do the words sound? Are they strong or weak? Do you feel relaxed, or do you feel tense? Although the exercise is an exaggeration, these are the same sensations that attorneys can experience when they go into the courtroom without preparing their voice.

The deep breath exercise teaches us where the work begins: it all starts with the breath. Now try this little exercise: Take a deep breath and hold it in for two seconds, then let it out slowly to a count of seven. Don't hold it in, but make sure that you take at least seven seconds to exhale. Do this several times. Now speak the same line again that you spoke before. What do you feel now? Is there more tension this time, or less? How does your voice sound this time, is it strong or is it weak? You see, it all begins with the breath.

In order to control the courtroom with your voice, you must first learn how to control your breath. Holding our breath is usually an unconscious reaction to fear. This is a "fight or flight" mechanism, preparing our bodies to listen for danger and deal with it. Back in the caves, we needed this instinctive, adrenaline response to escape death. But the body can't differentiate between the adrenaline rush that comes from a predator approaching your cave from the one that comes from speaking in public; the physical response is the same. The breath stops, just the same way. Now, as scary as jurors can be, we've never actually seen a jury *attack and eat* a trial lawyer. So this instinct can hurt more than it helps in the modern world, creating tension throughout the body and within the voice.

The actor's great secret—to controlling his voice, his body, his memory, his ability to connect with the other actors, the focus of the audience, his entire performance—is breathing.

Many people will hold their breath before they speak because they are afraid of saying the wrong thing, or are concerned with how their voice will sound. But what really happens when the advocate holds his or her breath? The first thing that happens is that the chest rises and there is tension. The vocal chords also become tense, and ultimately the mind becomes ill at ease. *Words need something to carry them, and that something is air.* The more air that is placed under the words in order to lift the sound, the more clear and solid is the voice, and when every word is carried with that same solid cushion of air, that phrase or sentence is conveyed to the listener with strength and confidence.

Abdominal breathing

The technique of abdominal breathing is vital if an advocate is going to speak with power and authority. Actually, this technique is not so much a new way of breathing as it is a re-learning of our natural way of breathing.

Baby's breath

Have you ever noticed that when a baby screams all night long he still has his voice in the morning? He doesn't lose his voice, as many adults do, no matter how much—and how loudly—he uses it. He can scream in a way that makes us adults cringe, thinking "That *must* hurt!" But, clearly, it doesn't. He can keep it up for hours, and then the next morning he doesn't have a scratchy, painful voice. He's ready to do it all over again.

This is because a baby breathes in a natural and unfettered way. He is using the breathing apparatus exactly as it was designed. Ineffective breathing is a learned behavior. For us truly to understand this, it is important first to understand exactly what abdominal breathing is.

Breathing is not initiated by our lungs. When you take a breath, the diaphragm (located directly below the sternum) expands, actually *pulling* air through your nose or mouth, down the trachea, and into your lungs. When you exhale, the diaphragm contracts, making your chest cavity smaller, and forcing the air from the lungs and back out through the same channels as mentioned before, right past your vocal cords. This an example of natural, relaxed breathing. But what do you think would happen if any part of this apparatus was blocked, or constricted?

The most common area of tension that gets in the way of our breathing is our abdominal muscles. From the moment vanity becomes a part of our life, we are taught to "stand up straight and suck it in." We are taught that to relax our belly is improper posture.

Exercise: Take a deep breath into your chest only. Do not allow your abdominal area to expand. Now recite the alphabet, increasing and decreasing your volume and pitch. Did you feel like you were holding your breath to make it to the end? Did you even make it to the end? Did you feel like you had control over your volume and voice? Did you like the tonal quality of your voice?

Now try the following abdominal breathing exercise. (review the enclosed CD-ROM for a demonstration of this exercise)

Exercise: Stand in front of a mirror with your feet shoulders' width apart. Place your hand on your belly directly below your sternum and above the bellybutton (the sternum is located in the center precisely where the hard portion of your ribs end). Relax your belly, and for the time being, imagine that you are breathing into the stomach area. Focus on allowing your breath to move your hand. Breathe in on a count of four and exhale on a count of eight. While doing this, watch your body. The only movement should be in your belly. Your shoulders should not rise and fall when you breathe. Concentrate on breathing directly into the abdominal area. The major sensation you should feel is the air coming through your mouth and your diaphragm rising and falling.

Now take another breath and exhale completely, but don't inhale. Don't let yourself inhale until your body does it for you—until you feel your diaphragm drop, pulling air into your lungs. Did you feel your abdomen "release"? Did you feel where the breath went (into your "stomach" area, not into your chest)? This is the way your body breathes when you are not controlling it. This is the most effective way for your body to take in air. If you are having a hard time breathing into your abdominal area, lie flat on your back and relax. As when you are asleep, you'll feel your abs relax, and you'll breathe properly, into your abdomen. Now repeat the exercise you did with the alphabet, but using your new technique of breathing into your abdomen.

Can you feel and hear the difference?

Vocal tone and volume

The voice is a very powerful emotional tool. It can make people laugh, cry, or cringe. It can inspire action, sympathy, or distaste. It can convey our most universal human emotions, or unmask hidden fears against our will.

To use your voice powerfully in the courtroom, you do not need to have the smooth, deep baritone of James Earl Jones. You do not need to have the vocal power of Pavarotti. You can have a lisp or a stutter. But you *do* have to have enough control over your voice to express yourself successfully and tell an emotional story. You *do* need to be heard by the trier of fact, and heard easily—if you force the judge or jurors to work hard to hear you, they will eventually give up. You need to have a voice that is pleasant—neither shrill nor rasping. You also need a voice that is strong and healthy enough to speak all day without becoming tired or scratchy, and losing all of this control.

The mechanics of the voice

When air is pushed out of the lungs by the contraction of the diaphragm, it passes through the trachea and past the vocal cords. The air causes the vocal cords to vibrate, producing sound. One common misunderstanding is that the vocal cords are responsible for the volume and tonal quality of your voice. The sound is initiated by the vocal cords, but is amplified by cavities of air in your face, head, neck, and chest, called resonators. These resonators are the "amplifiers" that allow Pavarotti to be heard all the way in the back row at Carnegie Hall. If you rely on your vocal cords to increase your volume, you will strain, and possibly lose, your voice.

Each resonating cavity is primarily responsible for amplifying different sounds and pitches. The higher cavities (in your head and face) are responsible for the higher pitches, and sounds like "eeee." The lower the cavity, the lower the pitch it resonates. For this reason, it is essential to develop the use of each resonating cavity. If you feel you have a flat, "colorless" voice, it is because you are not effectively employing each resonator. Have you noticed how flat your voice sounds when you get a cold? Have you noticed it usually sounds "lower" in pitch when your sinuses are clogged? That is due to the fact that the resonators in your head and face are not functioning. Using the complete range of resonators means the difference between a "mono" voice and a "stereo" voice. The exercises at the end of this chapter, and on the enclosed CD-ROM, will help you develop the resonating power of each of these cavities, to give you a "stereo" voice.

The vocal apparatus is like any other muscle: it must be exercised and trained to operate at peak efficiency. Done regularly, the warm-ups and exercises at the end of this chapter will help you earn a voice that is filled with color, responds to your wishes, and never lets you down.

Vocal warm-ups

In addition to the body, it is essential to warm up your voice. As stated in the "Vocal tone and volume" section above, your vocal quality is a vital element of your presentation. The following exercises are designed to relax and to strengthen the voice. Please read through this chapter, then review this material on the enclosed CD-ROM. Remember, while doing all vocal exercises, be sure that you are standing in what we call a neutral position: arms hanging at your side, feet shoulders' width apart. Please use the breathing techniques described in this course. *Improper breathing can cause injury to the vocal cords.*

As we mentioned in "The Mechanics of the Voice," the vibration of the vocal cords initiates the sound, but that sound is amplified and animated by the resonators—resonating cavities throughout your head, face, neck, and chest. Warming up and strengthening these resonators is essential for healthy, powerful, and enduring vocal quality.

Daily vocal humming

This exercise will dramatically increase your vocal power and the life of your voice. Please refer to the CD-ROM for a demonstration of this exercise.

1. Begin by humming a familiar song ("Happy Birthday," "Mary Had a Little Lamb," "Little Red Corvette," or any song that is familiar to you).

2. Progressively hum louder with each verse of the song. Now open your mouth wide and release your jaw, but *keep humming, not singing.* The sound should be exactly the same as it was with your mouth closed. If you are having trouble with this, try placing your tongue flat against the roof of your mouth. Make sure the sound is coming out of your nose, not your mouth.

3. Be sure that your jaw is relaxed. Tension in your jaw and neck can cause you to strain or injure your vocal cords.

4. Place your hand on your chin and jaw and hum through your nose, mouth open, hand on chin and jaw.

5. Increase your volume, until you can feel your sinuses vibrating.

6. Continue for 5 minutes.

This exercise, more than any other, can quickly improve the quality and strength of your voice. Done regularly, it can greatly extend the life of your voice. To get the most out of this exercise, you must hum loudly enough to feel the sound vibrating in your nasal cavities, and your jaw and neck must be relaxed. Practice this for one week—five minutes every day—and you will notice a marked difference in the quality of your voice.

Humming loudly will vibrate your sinus cavities, and after a few minutes it will cause them to drain. (This is a bonus for allergy sufferers and can help a lot if you have a cold.)

Resonators

These exercises will open up the resonating cavities in your body. First, spend a few minutes on each of the five sounds. When you feel like each sound is warming up the desired resonating cavity, put them all together. Start with the first sound, and go through each one consecutively on the same breath:

"MEE"

This sound should come from high up in your nose. It should be very nasal. It is designed to warm up your nasal cavities and those in your forehead, not to sound beautiful. If you can't feel it vibrating in your nose and forehead, you are not making the sound nasal enough. Try putting a pencil between your teeth (with the ends sticking out to either side of your mouth). Make the "MEE" sound again, and focus on sending the sound up and over the pencil.

"MAY"

This sound drops a bit to the middle of your face, where the sinus cavities are located. It is lower in your nose than MEE, but still above the teeth and very nasal.

"MA"

Now the sound is in your mouth, coming from your lips and tongue.

"MO"

This sound comes right from your throat. You should feel it in the area around your Adam's apple. Do not force the sound to be loud, just the vibration will do it.

"MOO"

By now, the sound is in your chest. You should feel the vibration in your chest cavity.

Putting voice and breath together

"HA, HA, HA"

Take a deep, abdominal breath. Now vocalize on a quick and loud "HA" sound, one single breath per "HA." You should feel your diaphragm area (the belly) pulsing, thrusting, and releasing with each sound. Be aware of any tension you may have in your body, especially the throat. Now exhale with a long "HA" sound on a count of eight. Pick a spot across the room and send the sound on a cushion of air to that spot.

"HO, HO, HO"

Now repeat the same exercise with the sound "HO." Be aware of what your mouth and throat are doing with this sound, as opposed to the "HA" sound. How are they different? How are they alike?

"HEE, HEE, HEE"

Now repeat the same exercise with the sound "HEE." How does this sound feel? What is happening with your mouth that is different from the other sounds? It should be more widely open in order to produce a clear sound

Releasing tension in your face

Squeeze your face tightly; scrunch it up really small, then release. We call this the "prune face." Now open the face wide as you can, stretching the tongue out as far as you can. This is called the "lion face." Now squeeze your face tightly again, and then open it wide. Squeeze, open. Squeeze, open. Now place your hands on your face right below each ear and start massaging your jaw muscles. Massage the muscles from the top of the jaw (below the ear) all the way along the jaw line.

Tongue twisters

Do you know what the strongest muscle in the human body is? The tongue! So, what would you do if you had an athletic event coming up that would work certain key muscle groups? You would train and exercise those muscles. The following tongue twisters are designed to help you exercise your tongue to help you improve your overall diction. Repeat aloud the following tongue twisters as quickly and as clearly as you can:

- Unique New York, Unique New York

- Toy Boat, Toy Boat, Toy Boat

- Red Leather, Yellow Leather

When you can do these three without trouble, try the ones on the list below! If you find yourself breaking into laughter, good! It is all part of warming up, and anything that "cracks you up" will help free you for a better performance.

- Mercurially
- Merkily Mercurially
- Trash Us, Thrash Us
- Minimally
- Minimally Ninny
- Young Onion
- Onion Reunion
- Syllable Sibilant
- Minimally Linearly
- Minimally Mimmy
- Young Onion Reunion
- Stitch Wish
- Presseth Precious
- Worthy Worthily

- Preface Precious Presseth
- Young Runyon Onion Reunion
- Linearly Literally
- Literally Literary
- Minimally Melanie
- Melody Melanie
- Minerally Milliner
- Mental Metal
- Minerally Millennium
- Linoleum Millennium
- Aluminum Millennium
- Lemon Aluminum Millennium
- Ghoul Girl

Putting all your vocal exercises together

Stand with feet shoulders' width apart and your arms hanging loosely by your side. Your head should be balancing on your body as if you had a string running from the base of your spine, through the top of your head to the top of the ceiling. This is the neutral position. Take a moment to breathe and relax in the neutral position.

Speak your opening argument with no movement, *i.e.*, no gestures, facial expressions, eyebrow lifting, and so on. When you feel tension creeping into your body, stop, breathe into the area of tension, release it, and begin again. This will force your emotion and expression into your voice. It is not easy, so keep practicing.

Chapter 3:
Vocal Inflection

We, as human beings, are very sensitive to tones of voice. For instance, when you talk to a baby, the baby does not understand the words you are saying but knows the emotion or intent of what you are saying from your tone of voice. Your choice of *inflection*—that is, which syllables are emphasized with a rise in pitch—can elicit a visceral reaction from your listener. One of the keys to keeping the jury captivated is to use the appropriate tone of voice to tell your story.

The inflection of your voice will tell someone whether they should listen to you or just not bother. It will tell those listening whether you respect the person to whom you are speaking. Since vocal inflection sends messages to the listener, learning the secrets of how to use vocal inflection is a top priority for an advocate.

At this point, we recommend that you review the "Vocal Inflection" section of the enclosed CD-ROM to hear the different inflections spoken out loud.

There are three common types of inflection:

Falling inflection

A falling inflection is the inflection we associate with a statement with a period at the end. It signals "the end." Finished. No more. Phrases such as "thank you" and "they all lived happily ever after." Think of the reaction you have if you walk into a shop and the clerk asks you an innocuous question such as "Can I help you?" If he says this with a falling inflection ("Can I help you."), what does it make you feel? You may get the impression that he doesn't really want to help you—that he's busy and you are really interrupting his day. But if he asks the same question with a rising inflection (a question mark at the end), it gives a very different impression: he *cares* about your needs and truly *wants* to help you. Speak that sentence out loud to yourself, first using a falling inflection ("Can I help you."), then using a rising inflection ("Can I help you?"). Can you hear the difference?

In court, a falling inflection is often over used by attorneys when asking simple questions such as "What is your name." "What do you do for a living." "Where were you on the night of December thirty-first." In an attempt to project an image of authority, to make the listener feel that "this is *fact*," many attorneys will use a falling inflection to excess. A question spoken with a falling inflection tells jurors that you either already know the answer, or that you don't care about the answer and neither should they. This may be a useful choice for you to make during cross-examination. The use of a falling inflection will imply your *suspicion* of the answer. But the constant use of falling inflections creates a rhythm which the listener will tune out. Have you ever noticed how sleepy you get on a train? The rhythm of the motion can put you to sleep, just as the rhythm of the rocking cradle will quiet a child. If you continue with a falling inflection, not only will you lose the jurors' interest, you will make them drowsy!

Rising inflection

A rising inflection is the one we most commonly associate with a question. It tells the listener that there is more to come or that you have asked a question and are waiting for a response. Answers to questions such as, "So you threw out the contract?" or "Then you signed the letter?" become much more important when the question is given a rising inflection. *A question asked with a rising inflection requires a response.*

In your opening statement or closing argument, using a rising inflection will generate a response in the mind of the jurors. If they hear "Life, liberty, and the pursuit of…?" with a rising inflection, they will automatically finish that sentence in their heads. What do you want the jurors to *say* in their heads? If Johnny Cochran said "If the glove doesn't fit …?" he would have twelve jurors saying silently "you must acquit."

In voir dire, your inflection tells the jurors how the process works, whether you want to have a conversation or a fact-checking session, and whether you really care about the answers you are given. Remember the different reaction you had when the shop clerk asked if he could help you, and put a rising inflection at the end of the question? It makes the question and the questioner seem less threatening, doesn't it? It communicates warmth, friendliness, and a genuine interest in the answer. Think of the ways in which your inflection can effect your relationship with the jurors. In voir dire, you will get more important information in less time if the jurors feel comfortable answering your questions. If they feel interrogated by falling inflections, they will be more likely to give you only "yes" or "no" answers. If you are "interrogating" a sympathetic witness on cross-examination, who looks like the bad guy? On the other hand, if you are dealing with a witness who is obviously hostile toward you, and you are asking your questions in a friendly way, who will the jury be more likely to respond to? What will the jury actually hear? Who will be persuasive?

Obviously, there are times when you want to deliver a monologue during cross-examination: when you are not asking polite questions, but making a series of statements for the witness to agree with. In that case, using a series of falling inflections helps you to do that. But be careful that you are not creating a rhythm with your inflections that will make it hard for the jurors to listen to your message.

Sustained inflection

A sustained inflection is the vocal pattern we commonly associate with a list. It is best used to link things together when we don't want to give the impression that we are finished speaking: "So when the defendant threw the rock across the fence … he couldn't see that there was a house … or that the house had windows on that side … or that … ." Even when the speaker stops speaking, the jury is left waiting for what he or she has to say next. If you leave them hanging with a sustained inflection—if you do not "finish" a statement with a falling inflection—the listener mentally finishes it for you. This can be very effective if you have engaged them enough in your story that they finish your statement in your favor. You have given them the power to affect the ending. (More on this later.)

A sustained inflection can also help you connect separate events in your listener's mind. If you are reciting a list of events and you speak as if every comma is a period, allowing your inflection to fall after each event, the individual events will stand out as separate events in the jurors' minds. However, if you sustain the inflection between each separate thought, those thoughts will be linked together for the jury. If you call your spouse from the office to ask him or her to pick up some groceries, would you recite each item with a falling inflection (with a period at the end)? No. You would use a sustained inflection to link the items together. Read the following sentences out loud, with a falling inflection after each item, and listen to how strange it sounds:

> Honey, would you stop by the store and pick up some groceries?
>
> We need milk.
>
> And cheese.
>
> And bread.
>
> And coffee.
>
> And apples.

Sounds silly, doesn't it? And yet, attorneys listen to other attorneys speaking in exactly that way in court, and it becomes a habit. Remember, if you want to link seemingly separate events together in the mind of your listeners, you must use a sustained inflection. If you use a falling inflection, even seemingly related events become separated for your listeners.

Vocal inflection exercise: Try telling a story (a paragraph or so is enough) without using a single falling inflection. Record yourself using a tape recorder. When you listen to the recording, you may find that speaking without falling inflections is much harder than it sounds. Obviously, we are not advocating that you never use a falling inflection. However, it is so commonly used in our daily speech (particularly that of attorneys), that we must practice speaking without it in order to take full advantage of all the methods of inflection available to us.

Vocal Thunder

Putting all of these things together—abdominal breathing, vocal strength, and vocal inflection—enables you to use your voice to command the room and control the picture being painted in the minds of your listeners. Mastering these skills allowed Martin Luther King, Jr. and John F. Kennedy to express the passion they felt in speeches that would become the benchmark against which all speeches are judged. But vocal thunder need not always be a loud thunderclap; sometimes it is a low rumble in the distance. Vocal thunder enables Garrison Keillor to draw his audience into his stories about Lake Wobegon. It enables you to have an intimate conversation with a juror in the first row and still be heard clearly by the judge, the court reporter, and the juror in the back row.

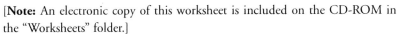

Vocal Thunder
Worksheet

[**Note:** An electronic copy of this worksheet is included on the CD-ROM in the "Worksheets" folder.]

Long-Term Goals:

1. List any vocal characteristics you would like to improve (vocal control, volume, strength, longevity, inflection, etc.):

   _____

   _____

2. List the techniques you intend to practice regularly to improve these characteristics:

   _____

   _____

3. Complete the vocal inflection exercise, using a tape recorder. What did you learn? Do you feel you need to practice these inflections regularly to make them more instantly accessible?

   _____

   _____

4. Notes, observations, and long-term results:

   _____

   _____

Case-Specific Work:

1. List the techniques you will use to warm up your voice in preparation for this case. (Are you breathing correctly—into your abdomen, instead of your chest?)

   _____

   _____

2. Are you using only falling inflections throughout, or are you adding color and meaning to your presentation with varied vocal inflections? List three key statements or questions in your case, and the inflection you find most effective for them.

   _____

   _____

3. Practice these inflections, using a tape recorder to make sure you are actually using the inflections you've chosen.

4. Notes and observations:

   _____

   _____

Chapter 4:
Why Your Body Sometimes Feels
As Though It Is Working Against You

Your body is the instrument with which you communicate with the judge, the jury, and even other attorneys. The gestures that you use, the way that you hold yourself, where you hold your hands, what you do with your face all give your "audience" a lasting impression of who you are. Extensive studies show that people make up their minds about another person within 30 seconds of being with them. This may sound extreme, but it is certainly true that we have a concrete first impression of another person by this time, and bad first impressions are notoriously difficult to overcome. Remember, concrete can be broken, but it requires a jackhammer.

There is a difference between perception and reality. If the reality is that you feel confident, honest, and relaxed in front of the jury, but the perception of the jurors, for whatever reason, is that you are nervous, dishonest, and uncomfortable, then you must change your body language to change the jurors' perception. The perception of the jury, right or wrong, is more important than your reality.

Question: Are you controlling your body, or is your body controlling you?

Recently, we were working with an attorney who felt that he gestured too much. When asked to elaborate upon this, he said that in law school one of his professors had told him that when arguing before a judge or jury, one should keep all movement to a bare minimum. The attorney is of Italian heritage, and he told us that everyone in his family "talks with their hands. It's a constant battle for me to keep my hands still. I hold them behind my back, I hold them together in front, but the truth is, I am very self-conscious about it. The last thing I should be thinking about when trying to present my case is 'Hey, how do my hands look!'"

Whenever we conduct a seminar and we ask how many people feel that they don't know what to do with their hands, or how many feel that their hands feel like cement blocks attached to their arms; inevitably, half of the people in the room raise their hands in agreement. (Then, we ask again, and up come the additional hands of people who were too self-conscious about their hand gestures to raise them the first time.) Why this unconscious fear of gesturing? Why are we afraid to involve our body in our presentation? Is there such a thing as gesturing too much?

The truth is that almost any movement is appropriate provided that it has a purpose. If you are moving your hands from side to side because you do not know where to place them, the resulting hand movements become distracting. However, if you move your hands with purpose—for example, in order to point out a person in the courtroom or perhaps to illustrate a point or an image—then your movement is an extension of your thought processes—or for our purpose, your storyline. The same is true not only of hand gestures but of all body movement. If, for example, in your storyline you are trying to convey the idea that a person was extremely stubborn or rigid, crossing your arms across your chest may be a great way to illustrate that without having to articulate it in words.

The basics of body language are vital for the advocate to understand. Do you know anyone who constantly crosses their arms in front of their chest? Or who repetitively flicks their hair out of their face? Or someone who cannot stand and talk to other people without leaning on a wall or a lectern? How about an attorney who seems trapped behind the counsel table, and not because the judge has ordered it?

The truth is that we all have these unconscious mannerisms, and they are usually a product of habit, fear—or even worse, both. Fear or discomfort is usually the environment in which our nervous habits appear.

There are no absolutes regarding gestures and movement. You can adjust your glasses a few times if you need to. You can clasp your hands behind your back a few times. You can put your hands in your pockets, or cross your arms, or push up your sleeves. But if these gestures become habitual, then they are getting in the way of your message.

We have all experienced the torture of standing in front of a group of people and feeling like our body is out to get us. Overcoming this problem requires rehearsal. Although some lawyers (or actors) may argue that rehearsing too much or memorizing their opening or closing will detract from their spontaneity, we believe quite the opposite is true. When you have practiced and prepared your presentation in front of a listener, or a coach or consultant, memorized and perfected the text for optimal effectiveness, you will actually have more freedom to improvise and to be spontaneous than if you were not prepared. When the jury joins you, remember that this is the first time that the *jury* has heard it, and your freshness and spontaneity comes from your being present in front of this group of people. Without fail, the best and most effective openings and closings that we have seen were memorized, rehearsed, and worked and re-worked. The attorney had lived with the words for so long that it gave them such a confidence and authority that the jury was compelled to listen.

If you know the text that well, then you are free to forget it—to know that it will come to you as needed. You can make adjustments—the sound of your voice, your word choice, the gestures you use, can all be modified because you know the text completely.

Joshua Karton recommends a wonder exercise, which has many applications: find a partner to serve as your "audience." Tell your opening statement to this audience without using your voice. Pantomime, gesture wildly—use anything but words to convey your story. When you have finished, ask your "listener" to repeat your story back to you, as he or she understood it. (Your partner is allowed to use words.) Still using only physical gestures yourself, fill in any vital information you failed to communicate to your partner the first time. This technique will not only make you a more natural, relaxed "gesturer," it will also lead you to discover many powerful gestures that you may want to use in court, to enhance your story.

David is an excellent criminal defense attorney. Although his opening statement was well written and thought out, David needed our assistance using physical gestures. His eye contact with the jurors was good, but he seemed to be cut off from the waist up. The jurors thought that he appeared stiff. After working with him on some exercises to free up his body, we discovered some gestures that would enhance his argument. In one part, he punched his open palm suddenly and with force when he was explaining how his client had been beaten. In another part, he clenched his fist to illustrate how his client had been choked. All of these gestures came when he let them come. We did not give them to him. He found them on his own. But most importantly, they enhanced and contributed to his argument. They did not detract from it.

Recall what we said earlier that one should only move with purpose. The same is true of gesturing in the courtroom. Your gestures should be a natural extension of what you are saying, your storyline. There's an old acting saying: "Don't just do something, stand there!" When a person who is not trained in the art of communication and presentation says that you gesture too much, most of the time what she means is that you are doing the same gesture over and over again; hence, the repetitiveness of the gesture has become distracting. Standing relaxed and still is better than gesturing nervously without intent or purpose.

But how do you know whether your gesture is appropriate? When are the times when less is more, where standing still is more effective? Is there such a thing as gesturing too much?

When you are preparing your opening or closing argument, there are four questions you should ask:

1. How does this affect my credibility with the judge and jury?

2. Do the gestures enhance or distract from my argument?

3. In this instance, is less more?

4. Does the gesture add or detract from my courtroom presence?

Movement and the use of space

Always move with purpose. Particularly when speaking to an audience or a jury, it is important that every move you make is conscious and an extension of your story. Walking and movement can effectively *enhance* your presentation. Actors who play attorneys on television walk around the courtroom. Why? Because their director knows that conscious movement can add importance to an issue and make a statement more interesting. The director has "blocked" (planned) that movement very carefully. Wandering aimlessly, or shifting from foot to foot, will not *enhance* your presentation; it will detract from its forcefulness.

The key to moving effectively in the courtroom is awareness. Few of us are aware of our nervous behaviors. Try these techniques to make yourself aware of your own nervous habits:

- Rehearse you story in front of a mirror—or better yet, a video camera.

- Ask for honest criticism from someone you trust and will listen to.

- Keep in mind that it is all right to move your hair away from your face or to put your hands in your pockets for a moment. But if these movements become habitual, the jury will *perceive* you as nervous and you will lose credibility with them.

- When in doubt, *don't just do something, stand there!*

The curse of the lectern

Of course, there will be times when you are arguing in federal court, or before a judge who chains you to a lectern or counsel table. This recent trend to prohibit lawyers from moving about in the courtroom is a response to the random, superfluous movements some advocates cannot restrain themselves from making. Some judges are worried that the lawyer will "take over the courtroom." If you use all movement in a conscious, meaningful way, you reduce the chance that it will annoy the judge and that he or she will force you to stand still. If you are required to stay *at* the lectern, *do not stay behind it.* We know that the lectern creates a sense of security: you don't need to worry about your hands, your notes are there, the microphone is there, and so on. But the lectern creates a visual block between you and the jurors. It makes your presentation much more formal, and makes it nearly impossible for you to communicate *with* them as one of them. It separates you from them, literally and figuratively.

If you happen to be "vertically challenged," as Lisa is at 5'3", the lectern becomes an even greater problem. You can't use gestures to enhance your argument and clarify your picture because your hands can't be seen above the lectern. You look small, and you become a talking head.

If you must be at the lectern, you can nearly always eliminate the barrier while maintaining the benefits of the lectern by taking just one step. For example:

- If the judge is directly in front of you and the jury is to your left, take one step backward. From the judge's perspective, you are still behind the lectern. From the jurors' perspective, you are not. And you still have your notes, your water, and the microphone a mere step away.

- If the lectern is set up in such a way that the jury is directly in front of you, take one step to the side, off the back corner of the lectern. Again, all of the benefits of the lectern are still available to you, but you have eliminated the barrier between you and the jurors.

Body warm-ups

On opening night, a professional actor does not stand around rehearsing his lines. Instead, he tunes his "instrument": he warms up his body and voice. A good actor knows his lines cold; he is prepared with his text. A good actor also knows that if he forgets his lines, he will be okay. He knows the story. And so it should be with the advocate. You have been living with your story for months, perhaps even years. When you simply tell your story, there is no such thing as losing your place.

Many attorneys tell us that they feel physically and vocally relaxed by the second or third day of trial, but the first day is one big haze of nervous tension. Given the fact that your first impression will be established in voir dire and during your opening statement, the third day may be too late to fix a negative first impression.

A simple warm-up helps you release the tension that prevents you from honestly communicating with your listeners. It also gives you the benefit of "beginning" your presentation before you even walk into the courtroom. Thus, you are not beginning your performance the first time you stand up to speak; you are merely continuing the process that you started in your car on the way to the courthouse.

Body warm-up exercises

The exercises on these pages and the enclosed CD-ROM, help release the tension we all hold in certain parts of our body. If you succeed in releasing the tension, your body functions as one unit. Your hands become an extension of your body and emotions, instead of useless distractions that make you self-conscious.

When warming up your body, find a place where you will not feel self-conscious, a few floors up from the courtroom perhaps. Always remember not to stretch too far when you are warming up. If you feel any pain or discomfort, *stop*. Always breathe correctly. Use your breath to enhance a stretch; your muscles can't work without oxygen, and you can't relax without breathing. Also try to remember that when you are stretching any part of your body, relax the rest of it. For example, don't relax your neck while placing undue tension in your shoulders or arms. Try the following exercises:

Tense and release

The basic tense and release exercise is something you can do virtually anywhere, even in the courtroom. People will not know that you are preparing your body for performance.

1. Make a fist. Squeeze hard, feeling the tension rise from your hand all the way to your shoulder.

2. Now release.

3. Repeat and release. Notice how much more relaxed that area of your body is.

4. Repeat, using your feet, shoulders, and abdominal muscles.

Head rolls

1. Stand up straight, feet shoulders' width apart. Imagine that there is a string running from the base of your neck straight through the top of your head.

2. Now let your head drop down in front of you, chin to your chest. Be sure not to tense your neck. Your head

should just be hanging in front of you. Take a minute to feel the stretch, then slowly raise your head back to center.

3. Drop your head to the right; again, be sure that you are not tensing other parts of your head, neck, or body. Take a moment to feel the stretch, then slowly let your head rise back to center. Do not lift it up, but instead feel it "float" back to center, hovering on top of your neck.

4. Repeat this motion on the left side, ending with your head back to center.

5. Now let your head fall in front of you and slowly roll to right, then back down in front; then left, then back down in front, and the slowly rising back to center.

6. Repeat this sequence several times, taking approximately five minutes.

Shoulder rolls

1. Stand up straight, with your feet shoulders' width apart.

2. Take a deep breath and exhale slowly, remembering to breathe into your abdomen. Do this a few times.

3. On your next breath, slowly raise your shoulders up to your ears as you inhale slowly, hold for five seconds, then exhale. At the same time, let your shoulders drop and release.

4. Do this several times.

5. Resume the neutral position, with your feet shoulders' width apart, and roll your shoulders back in a circular motion, returning to neutral. Repeat this movement for about one minute. Now reverse the roll, doing the same motion.

Arm swings

1. Stand up straight, with your feet shoulders' width apart.

2. Roll your shoulders and swing your arms, reversing direction every ten swings. Slowly stop swinging until you return to neutral. Take a deep breath and relax.

Drop-downs and roll-ups

1. Stand up straight, with your feet shoulders' width apart.

2. Slowly drop your head, chin to toward your chest. Continue dropping until your fingertips touch the floor. *Bend your knees if you must. Do not stretch further than your body will allow.*

3. Feel the stretch in your lower spine and your hamstrings.

4. Take an inventory of your body: Is your head relaxed, hanging freely from your neck? Are you letting the weight of your head pull you towards the floor? Are your arms hanging freely? Let go of all tension you notice in your body.

5. Now slowly roll up, starting from the base of your spine and stacking each vertebrae on top of the other, with the last to rise being your head.

6. Imagine a string attached to the top of your head, pulling you skyward.

7. Take a deep breath and repeat.

Body Language
Worksheet

[**Note:** An electronic copy of this worksheet is included on the CD-ROM in the "Worksheets" folder.]

Long-Term Goals:

1. List any aspects of your body language or movement that you would like to improve (gesturing, use of the podium or lectern, movement, lack of movement, shifting from foot-to-foot, etc.):

   _____

   _____

2. List the techniques you intend practice regularly to improve these characteristics:

   _____

   _____

3. In daily life, become aware of your body language and posture. Do you have any "habits" which may not be effective in the courtroom? What gestures do you use when speaking passionately about something outside of the courtroom? Which of those gestures would be effective in the courtroom?

   _____

   _____

4. Ask other people what they think about your body language. Write down any helpful comments. Ignore comments that aren't helpful!

_____

_____

Case-Specific Work:

1. List at least three exercises you have used to warm up your body so it is ready to assist you in expressing your story, rather than hindering you.

_____

_____

2. Rehearse your opening statement using only gestures. Write down any gestures you discover that you may want to incorporate into your presentation.

_____

_____

3. Notes and Observations:

_____

_____

Chapter 5:
Using Eye Contact To Build Relationships

"Group eye contact" does not exist. It is not possible to look at more than one person at a time. Effective eye contact involves looking at one person at a time, connecting with that person, and sharing information with that one person before moving on.

How does it feel when you are talking to someone and they are not looking at you? Most of us feel that such a person is hiding something, is not being truthful, or is shifty. We also feel that we must not be important to them if they don't have the common courtesy to look at us when they're speaking. Although this may seem elementary, many of us take for granted the importance that eye contact plays in making a human connection. Basic eye contact begins to bond you with your listener. It is the foundation of a relationship. For an attorney, it means the difference between talking *at* your jury and talking *with* them.

Taking time to look

In order to establish proper eye contact, you must first take the time to look at the person you are talking to. Most people, when asked to "make eye contact" in our seminars, begin by trying to look at every eye in the room in the first ten seconds. They roam over each person's eyes in what we call the "typewriter phenomenon"—usually moving from left to right, front row to back. They are *looking* at everyone, but *connecting* with no one.

When you decide to look a juror in the eye, you must:

- *Look:* See the person you are talking to. Take your time and make this connection. It will help keep you centered, and give your listener the impression that you are saying something important and that you feel *the listener* is important, too.

- *Acknowledge:* Acknowledge that you have made contact.

- *Speak:* Start talking *to* your listener.

Make sure that you take the time to look.

Practice the following exercise with everyone you come into contact with for one day (family, colleagues, clients). You'll notice how much more effectively you are communicating with, and listening to, people in this type of conversation.

Exercise: Before you start to speak, make eye contact and count to three. It will feel very awkward and unnatural, but it won't look so. If you are speaking to more than one person, finish a thought (not necessarily an entire sentence—you don't want to stare at them like a psychopath) with one person, look at the next person, count to three, then continue. Trust us with this one. If you can do this with your jury panel, you will be far more effective in your persuasion.

Messages sent with eye contact

Eye contact conveys honesty, confidence, respect, interest, and courtesy. Effective eye contact can mean the difference between a "speech" and a "conversation." *Lawyer Man* scans the room, connecting with no one. A persuasive trial lawyer connects with one person at a time, creating a conversation and building a relationship with each juror.

Obviously, it is possible to look someone right in they eye and lie. Nonetheless, in American and Canadian culture, the perception is that if you are telling me the truth you'll look me in the eye. If you are not able or willing to make effective and meaningful eye contact, the assumption is that you may be hiding something, fudging the truth, or worse.

You can also use eye contact, or the lack of it, to purposefully convey disrespect. If, on cross, you wish to imply disrespect or no interest for the answer, you can convey that by looking elsewhere. If you finish the question without retaining eye contact with the person you are questioning, you are diminishing the value that you place on the answer. You can use this deliberately to make a witness uncomfortable and to convey distrust or lack of interest in their testimony. Be careful; if you use this technique with a sympathetic witness, you may become the "bad guy" in the eyes of the jury. Use this technique consciously, and not out of fear.

Spend some time watching people engaged in conversation. Notice the way they use eye contact. When two people are speaking one-on-one, the person who is listening will maintain eye contact with the speaker. The person who is speaking should take responsibility for breaking the eye contact before he or she looks like a psychopath, because eye contact is very intimate and must be broken every few moments to avoid making the listener uncomfortable. In a one-on-one conversation, the speaker will break eye contact by looking at the floor, or across the room. But in a public speaking situation, the speaker should break eye contact with one person by looking at another person.

For the most part, everything you say to the jury should be said while making eye contact with one of your listeners. This doesn't mean you never look down or look away. But make it a goal to always be connecting with someone.

Many attorneys we work with tend to look down at the floor, or otherwise break contact with the jurors, when they are thinking about what to say next. This becomes their "tell," in poker terms. It tells the jury that you're not sure where you're going next, and that you're retreating from them to think about it. Try to maintain your connection with the jurors while you compose your thoughts. That tells the jurors that you and they are still in it together—that you're thinking about what you are about to say, which is perfectly normal, but you're courageous enough to stay *present* while you do it. Many of our clients resist trying this. They think they will feel too vulnerable, or that they will look bad. But once they have tried it, they realize the power of it. Once they are able to maintain their connection with the jurors and trust that the words will come, they realize that everything is *easier* with that connection.

If you absolutely must look away, do it in a moment of silence. Then look up and reconnect with your listeners before you resume speaking.

More time

Even when speakers realize the importance of making a connection with one listener at a time, most of them do not spend more than a second or two with each person. To build a relationship, you must spend *more time* with each juror before you move on to another. The amount of time you spend will vary, depending upon the listener and the importance of what you are saying. For instance, when you are quickly moving through something light, you might spend a few seconds with one person before you move to the next. But if you are discussing a very important point and you want to make sure the point is heard, and the weight of it felt, you might spend five or ten seconds with one person—enough to finish your point with that one person, so you do not diminish the weightiness of the statement by moving your eyes around the room. This does not mean you stare one person down until you have made your entire argument. It means that you finish a *thought* with one person, then another thought with another person. If you are making contact with Juror Number Three, rest assured that the other 11 jurors are receiving the information as well, with the added credibility that comes from the *relationship* being built between you and Juror Number Three.

When you feel that you have made your point or that you have established a real and human connection with a juror, you should complete your thought, make contact with someone else, and establish a new relationship.

Engaging the reluctant juror

There are occasions when eye contact is inappropriate. There may be jurors who simply are not comfortable with eye contact. If you notice this, don't take it personally; some people simply aren't comfortable with eye contact. They're used to being uncomfortable, and they won't dislike you for your initial attempt to make contact with them.

If you attempt to make eye contact with a juror and he or she just will not look at you, we are not suggesting that you stand there staring until he or she does look at you. Please choose someone else to whom to convey your message. Invite the reluctant juror into your conversation with the occasional glance, but do not force eye contact on anyone. Chances are, the person who is reluctant to make contact with you will forget about that uncertainty before you are finished.

Where you look

Where do we look when we connect with an individual? Do we look at the face? The eyes? The mouth? Do we try to avoid eye contact, in order to avoid offending? At one time or another, we have heard teachers and trainers tell students to do all of the above. What we tell our students and clients is focus both your eyes on *one* of the other person's eyes.

> **Exercise:** Stand face to face with another person about a foot apart looking into each other's

eyes. Your left eye should line up with her right eye, and your right eye should line up with her left eye. Notice, however, that it is impossible to *focus* on both of her eyes at the same time. Most human beings simply cannot do it. Even if we feel that we're doing it, it is not nearly as focused as we want it to be.

Now try focusing both of your eyes on *one* of her eyes. See how much easier it is? More importantly, your gaze is clear and focused. If you use this technique in the courtroom, your *attention* will also appear to the jury to be clearly focused on the other person.

How to focus attention in the courtroom

When you are in charge in the courtroom, where you focus your attention is where your listeners will focus their attention. Everyone is aware of the "tricks" you can employ to convey an impression of a witness by where you stand in the courtroom. Some attorneys stand near the jury box during direct to encourage their witness to look toward the jury. Other attorneys we've worked with use this technique on cross, because they feel that having an opponent's witness look *toward* but not *at* the jurors makes the witness look shifty. We believe that making the jurors look where you want them to, and conveying a certain impression of a particular witness, doesn't depend on where you are standing in the courtroom. If you have established yourself as the person to whom the jurors look for answers, then where you *look* is just as important as where you stand.

For example, if you want to convey a distrust of the answer, or a lack of respect for the testimony, look *only* at the jury (not at the witness) when asking the question. It may seem unnatural, but the jurors accept the convention, and it encourages them to look at *you,* and not at the witness. When you want the jury to look at the witness, focus your attention on the witness.

If you want the witness to look at the jury—and he or she has forgotten these instructions—you can lead his or her gaze as well. If he or she is answering a question and looking at you as you shift your gaze to look at the jury, the witness will follow your lead. Usually, witnesses remember your previous instructions at this point, but even if they don't, they still end up speaking to the jury.

NOTE: Make sure that you have already instructed your witness to look at the jury (in their eyes) and that he or she is capable of making effective eye contact. Better yet, give the witness the opportunity to *practice* this before testifying (See Chapter 12).

When you want the witness to look away from the jury, look directly at the witness when asking your question. If you do not look at the jury, chances are the witness will forget to, as well. Remember to prepare your witnesses for this technique from opposing counsel. If you want your witnesses to look at the jury, you must prepare them to *remember* to disengage themselves from the opposing counsel on cross-examination. This must be done thoughtfully. Witnesses who turn robotically to look toward the jury will appear awkward. But, if the witness is taught to turn to the jury out of a sincere need to tell the jurors his story, he will look strong and credible (See Chapter 12).

Another Hint: If you have a witness with a quiet, shy voice, position yourself near the juror farthest from the witness. He or she will instinctively speak up so you can hear the answers. This way you can be sure the entire jury can hear and understand the testimony.

Eye Contact
Worksheet

[**Note:** An electronic copy of this worksheet is included on the CD-ROM in the "Worksheets" folder.]

1. Are you making eye contact with your listeners, or are you locked on your notes or scanning the jurors' eyes indiscriminately?

   _____

   _____

2. Are you *taking the time to look* in voir dire, establishing contact before asking your questions and giving the other person time to expand on his or her answer?

   _____

   _____

3. List at least 3 key moments in which solid, steady, and focused eye contact is important to make your point.

   _____

   _____

4. Notes and Observations:

   _____

   _____

Part 2

Captivate The Jury Through The Power Of Storytelling

"Great trial lawyers are storytellers, explainers, raconteurs."

— James W. McElhaney

"Give me the story—please, the story."

— Gerry Spence

"The jury wants to hear a story. They're hard-wired for it."

— Joshua Karton

"Storytelling reveals meaning without committing the error of defining it."

— Hannah Arendt

Chapter 6:
Painting A Clear Picture

What if a painter walked up to you with a palette of colors—fiery reds, deep blues, bright yellows—and she said, "Look at this beautiful painting! I can see it right there! Isn't it wonderful?" You would say, "Oh, I don't know yet. The colors are pretty, but I don't see the painting."

Too many lawyers begin their opening statement with *facts* or points of law that they know are legally important to the case. This is like presenting all the colors on the palette and expecting your audience to "see" the same painting you see.

If you haven't told them *what happened* first, they have no framework from which to view this list of legal information. Obviously, you need to get certain facts into the record. However, you should tell your client's story *first*, so they know what each fact means and how to relate it to the story. Remember: during the first few minutes, the jury is eager to learn what the case is all about. They are eager for the *story.*

What's in a story? A story transcends a basic fact pattern and lets the listener become personally involved. A story is non-threatening. A great story is honest and leaves the listener wanting more.

"I'm getting to that, but first you need to understand contracts law..."

Many of our clients have had this conversation with us:

Lisa: Okay, we're four minutes into your opening, and I still have no idea what this case is about.

Attorney: I'm getting to that, but first you have to understand the principles behind ERISA.

Honestly, we don't need to understand that first. We need to know what happened, we need to know the story. Then we'll understand what you mean, and why it matters, when you tell us about the principles behind ERISA.

There is much discussion in trial advocacy about a University of Chicago study that concluded that 80 percent of jurors decided their verdict by the end of opening statements. Interestingly, this study never happened. Nonetheless, it has become the stuff of legend. In reality, it is unlikely that your opening statement will go so far as to *win* the case for you, but clearly, a bad opening statement can go a long way toward losing it.

Jurors interpret and deliberate the evidence *in the context of the story.* In other words, the *story* is the very essence of oral advocacy. The story provides a familiar point of view from which the jury can examine the evidence; if they examine the evidence from the viewpoint of your story, they are clearly more likely to decide in your favor. Opening statements are commonly referred to as the "puzzle," and the testimony and evidence as the "puzzle pieces." The "big picture" comes not from the opening statement as a whole but from your client's story, contained within your opening. Most trial lawyers are familiar with the adage that juries don't decide on just the facts, they decide on emotion and make the facts fit their story.

> "Instead of some standard words about opening statements, give them the theory of the case—carefully distilled into a memorable theme that will stay with them and shape their understanding throughout the trial."
>
> — James W. McElhaney, Trial Notebook

What is a good story?

A good story speaks to the average person. A good story is expressed in language that makes sense to the listener and is not cluttered with legalese. The storyteller must have a need to tell the story. The storyteller must have something important to say, something urgent that must be conveyed. A good story makes the listener feel emotionally involved. A good story expresses the pain and the need that your client felt when he first walked into your office asking for help. But by the time you have gone through years of motions, investigations, causes of actions, and depositions, a simple human story has often been replaced by a "fact pattern."

Show, don't tell

One of the biggest mistakes we see attorneys make is trying to tell the jurors what they should think.

Attorneys often want to argue in their opening statement; after all, they want to take full advantage of that time to begin to persuade the jurors that their cause is the right one. That's a great intention, but at such an early point in the trial, you don't yet have the credibility to tell jurors what to think. The jurors start thinking, "Stop trying to convince me—I haven't even heard any evidence yet! Let me come to my own conclusions. Don't try to put one over on me." Watching mock jurors deliberate has shown us just how sophisticated jurors are; they are wary of someone who tries to tell them what to think.

Are we suggesting that you should just "go with the flow" or just lay out the facts? No. We want you to take control of the picture from the very beginning. We want the jurors to put the pieces together using your picture like the cover of a puzzle box. However, you don't get there by telling them what to think. You get there by showing them what happened.

If you're representing the defense, don't tell the jury, "The plaintiff spent over an hour in that room with the contract, so we know she read it thoroughly before she signed it." Tell the jury, "The plaintiff took over an hour with the contract. Finally, she made the decision to sign it." While you're saying this last part, use pantomime body language—looking thoughtfully at a contract, thinking for a moment, and confidently signing the paper.

If you want the jury to understand that the plaintiff did *not* look at the contract before she signed it, you may not want to say that now—especially if it is a disputed fact. To do so makes you appear argumentative. Instead, as you say that "she signed the contract," show *how* she signed it: pantomime her quickly grabbing the contract, scratching off a signature without looking at it, and thrusting it back to someone. It doesn't have to be a big movement, but it has to be specific enough to create a clear picture. When we've interviewed jurors, we found that they incorporate this data as part of the picture. This example was used in a mock trial; during deliberations, the jurors said, "Well, she didn't even look at the contract." That sentence had never been uttered during the presentation, but because the attorney had portrayed the action in that way, they assumed it was a fact.

How to use analogies to explain complicated information

Analogies help the jury relate to your story. They also help clarify important technical information so that jurors can make sense of it. If you have complicated facts for the jury to analyze, tell them a simple story that clarifies the principles involved. For instance, say you're defending a bank that is being sued by XYZ Corporation. The former CEO of the company embezzled a large sum of money from corporate accounts that he opened at your client's bank and there is a dispute over whether the CEO even had the authority to open the corporate accounts in the first place. Your evidence involves the corporation's ledgers, the corporate resolutions on file at the bank, 15 accounts, corporate profits from these accounts, a complicated chain of command, industry standards, and "reasonable diligence." Most jurors are going to be totally lost, and you know it. How do you make them understand *why* none of these actions were the bank's fault?

Tell them a story that emphasizes your theme, which is that the heads of this corporation allowed the embezzlement to happen on their watch and now they're trying to pass the buck (pun intended). Look for a story from your own life that exemplifies this theme. We had a client with a similar case who used, with great success, the following analogy.

> When I was 13, my father asked me to make a deposit for him while he was at work. He gave me $200 in cash, and I was supposed to walk to the local bank and put it into his account. On the way to the bank, I passed the bike store. There in the window was the red ten-speed I'd been asking my parents for ever since my friend Jimmy got one for his birthday. It was on sale for $175. Well, I never made it to the bank. I hid the bike behind a box in the garage before my dad got home. Unfortunately, my dad backed the car into that box, and my new bike, the very next day. "Where did the bike come from, Bob?" he asked me. "Somebody gave it to me," I lied pitifully. "Where's the deposit slip from the bank, Bob?"
>
> Well, I spent the next six months mowing lawns and weeding yards to repay that $200. My dad was angry, and he punished me. He did not, however, try to sue the bike store for selling me the bike! That would be ludicrous, wouldn't it? He had given me the responsibility for that money, and I blew it.

My dad took his responsibility for the loss, and he made me take mine. It wasn't the bike store's fault!

That's what this case is about. XYZ Corporation is trying to sue the bike store!

Now you've given the jury a context from which to view the complicated facts and testimony to come. Now you can explain why the bank isn't liable, and it all can be related to this story. The key is, you must keep relating back to this story. You must tell them who in that story represents which principal in your case. You must keep the analogy alive for them.

Once you have developed an analogy that clarifies your argument, put on your devil's advocate hat and try to poke holes in it. For example, in the analogy about the bike store, the plaintiff's attorney might stand up and say:

> "Nice story, ladies and gentlemen. But in this case the owner of the bike store ran out onto the sidewalk, pulled the kid in by the arm, gave him candy, and promised him that his father would never know. He pressured the kid to buy the bike. So the bike store deserves to be held accountable!"

In our client's case, the facts would not have supported that counter-attack. The analogy worked perfectly. With a different set of facts, the analogy might have backfired. Do your best to destroy the analogy before you decide it's that the one you're going to bet your opening statement on.

Here's one of our favorite examples of opposing counsel using your analogy against you:

Defense closing:

The plaintiff is trying to take your eye off the ball. Whatever you do, keep your eye on that ball.

Plaintiff's rebuttal:

Mr. Jones is right. Keep your eye on the ball. And hit it out of the park.

Also remember—an analogy should enhance the clarity of your story or your theme. It should not replace your clear explanation of the issues involved in your case. An analogy does not give you a "way out" of having to explain clearly, for example, how an internal combustion engine works. It just gives you a tool with which to reinforce your clear explanation. Try to find a simple, clear explanation that does not include an analogy *first,* then look for an analogy to reinforce that explanation.

How to make technical testimony interesting

Tell the jury how technical testimony fits into your story. Remember that in every case there is a story. Something happened. If you present your case as a story rather than as legal theory, the jurors will attempt to fit the technical testimony and facts into that story.

If your client's story is not something the jury can readily relate to, use an analogy to give the jury a simple story to which they can relate especially complex technical facts.

You must become the jurors' advocate in the courtroom. Ideally, your witness should try to explain the technical information in terms that the layperson can easily understand, but you must realize that the responsibility of ensuring that the jury does understand rests on you. If you explain to them what the testimony means and how it fits into your overall story of the case, they will make the effort required to understand it.

Condensing your story to its basic elements

Six Sentences

If you had only a few sentences with which to tell your story to the jury, what words would you choose?

> "He breached the contract terms." *OR* "He *broke* his *promise*."

> "She died as a result of her wounds." *OR* "She was *slaughtered*."

> "He committed spousal abuse." *OR* "He *violently raped* his wife."

Write down six *short* sentences to tell your story, as if those were the only six you had. These sentences can't be paragraphs in and of themselves. No semicolons. Remember, this is not your entire opening statement, just your client's story. The six sentences don't even need to be grammatically correct. They should just describe what happened in the most efficient and effective way possible to engage the emotions of the jury. Structure them with a beginning, a middle, and an end. Make sure that the last sentence asks for the ending you want. For example, if you were prosecuting the O.J. Simpson case, your six sentences might look like this:

1. He repeatedly beat, raped, and tortured his wife for years.

2. When she left him, he stalked her, threatened her, and finally ambushed her at her home.

3. He lay in wait and viscously slashed and butchered her.

4. Tell him that being a star doesn't mean he can get away with murder.

5. Don't let him mutilate our legal system like he mutilated her body.

6. Punish him for her.

If you were defending Simpson, you might come up with this:

1. O.J. Simpson is a loving father and a national hero.

2. As he mourned for the wife he loved, some crooked, racist cops decided to play judge and jury.

3. Since they don't have any evidence, they framed him because they just don't like him.

4. Tell the cops that they can't get away with twisting the facts to make themselves look good.

5. Don't let them make O.J. into another victim in this tragic case.

6. Free him.

Tell your story to a child

If common sense and confidentiality permit, tell your story to a child. If that is not possible, tell your spouse or someone who is not an attorney. That person will bring up questions that will help you discover what is truly important in the story: "So was she hurt?" "But what did she do to him?" "Why was she driving so fast?" The questions of a non-attorney will help you distill your case to its essentials. All of the evidence becomes important because it confirms your theme.

Tell your story in pantomime

Lock yourself in your office and tell your story to an imaginary "audience" through pantomime. We know it feels silly, but you can find gold with this exercise. First, you'll find it very hard to pantomime legalese, and you'll discover the simplest, most basic elements of the story. Further, this exercise will help you put yourself in your client's shoes, and you may discover emotional elements of the story that you didn't think about before.

Tell it like it is, and leave them wanting more

When it comes right down to it, we need your story, *warts and all.* Jurors are much more sophisticated than they were even five years ago. They're not just watching courtroom dramas like

Matlock and *L.A. Law* anymore. Now they're watching Court TV and reality programming. They are sick to death of salespeople, politicians, and anyone else who tries to pull the wool over their eyes, fudge the truth, or leave out details they don't like. They know you have an agenda. Their "B.S. meters" are at full tilt, and they are ready to catch you in what they consider a lie.

Don't justify their distrust. Tell them the truth—they can take it. Think of Rudy Giuliani after the 9/11 attacks. He seemed to be the only person who was willing to tell us the whole truth, warts and all. Regardless of our politics, he captivated us as a nation and earned our trust.

Take control of your bad facts; don't try to run away from them

Whether a judge or juror, the trier of fact always appreciates the one who's going to give them the whole truth. This means you must embrace the bad facts of your case and put them out in front. Would you rather be viewed by the jury as an honest advocate or as a slick spin doctor? The answer is obvious.

We're always amazed at how difficult it is for attorneys to "admit" the warts in their case. Sometimes it is the week before trial when they finally admit to us that there's a memo floating around out there saying, "We have to make sure that our shareholders never get wind of this," or "Everyone was drunk or stoned in the car when it crashed."

A jury needs to sense that you are the one who will always "tell it like it is." To convey that sense in your presentation, you must be fully committed to the truth. You must outwardly respect the intelligence of the triers of fact. The scariest warts are less scary when we admit to them with confidence. If the jurors believe that you will admit the worst, then they are more likely to believe you when you tell them why those warts don't matter.

Leave them wanting more

When you have built that credibility with the jurors, they find themselves looking to you to make sense of the information they hear. Again, the effect is similar to what happened after 9/11: whenever a televised news conference came on and Mayor Giuliani was about to speak, in living rooms all across the country someone would tell everyone else to be quiet, then turn up the television to hear what he had to say.

How do we demand that kind of attention in the courtroom? It all comes down to structure, structure, and more structure. The story told must be complete and detailed, with new moments and revelations at every turn. Playwrights have an old adage: every time a door opens onstage, something new has to happen to further the story. In a courtroom, try to commit that every new "character" will cause some new information to be learned. Your story is being told not just through opening statements and closing arguments, but through direct and cross-examination as well. It's not enough to show them what you told them you would in opening. It needs to be built on surprise and revelation.

For example, instead of telling the jurors in your opening statement exactly what a certain piece of evidence will prove, it might be more effective to simply tell them that they "will see a very important memo about X ... More about that document later ... ." A great story builds in new and interesting revelations at every opportunity, leaving the jury always wanting more.

How to inspire your audience

How to inspire? Every trial lawyer dreams of doing it: dreams of standing in front of the jury, looking in to each juror's eyes, all of them captivated in the silence of the lawyer's presence. The great attorney doesn't start by saying, "Ladies and gentlemen, before you can understand what happened to Ms. Smith, you have to understand the way the Americans with Disabilities Act works." Instead, she starts by saying, "Ladies and gentlemen, we are here because ABC Communications Company refuses to take responsibility for the actions of their managers." The jurors are relieved—they think, "We actually might hear something interesting." The lawyer goes on to tell a story about what ABC did to her client, but while listening to this engaging story we feel that this attorney is talking about something that is clearly very important to her. Even though this story is about what happened to her client, it feels as if it might have happened to anyone; it might have happened to someone we care about. As the storyteller goes on, she shifts gears, and all of a sudden we are asked to think about certain issues. This story is like a great film, for we are engrossed in the story, we care about the characters, and yet we are also examining how we think and feel about certain core values and beliefs that we hold. We don't mind looking this deep inside ourselves, for the story helps us do that without getting too close. It's our safety net. We can feel, we can laugh, and we can even cry, but somehow we're safe in this story.

When the story is over, the great attorney looks at the jurors and asks them to make a decision. She says to them, "What will you do?" We are engaged, and suddenly we feel very alive. We feel important again, all thanks to the storyteller.

What exactly is inspiration? Is it some ethereal gift from the cosmos, bestowed on the select few, or is it a product of pure luck? Did she just happen to be really "on" that day?

Often, when we speak of someone being inspirational, we find ourselves at a loss for words. All that we know is that we felt something real inside, perhaps something that led us to see a certain person or situation in a completely different way. We were influenced; we were inspired. We say to ourselves, "Wow, that person really has a gift!" But in reality, the true storyteller is purposefully trying to affect the listener. It is not some gift from the cosmos, but a specific action plan with an end result in mind. Whether it is a screenplay, an opening statement, a speech, or a father teaching a lesson to his child, when done effectively the action plan is present.

Webster defines *inspiration* as "the action or power of moving the intellect or emotions." All effective stories, such as the one described above, are rooted in action: the action of moving the intellect and emotions, and the act of influencing or suggesting opinions. In other words, inspiring the jury or your audience or the trier of fact is an active process. It is something that you *do* to someone else.

In order to inspire, we must actively talk to the emotion or intellect. Even when talking to the intellect, we are still talking to the emotion, for the listener in this case has weighted his or her emotional response in the intellect. The best way to speak the language of emotion is through the act of constructive storytelling. Think about the most inspirational speakers that you've ever heard: Martin Luther King, Jr.; John F. Kennedy; Ronald Reagan; and Bill Clinton, just to name a few. Regardless of whether you agree with their messages, they all spoke to us through the heart and through our emotions. JFK often stirred in us the emotion of civic duty and patriotism, while Dr. King stirred in us the emotion of injustice and faith in our higher selves. What they all have in common, however, is that they all called us to *action*.

The next time that you're composing your opening statement or closing argument remember the following:

1. What emotional response do I want the trier of fact to feel?

2. What specific action do I want them to perform?

3. Is my case being told in the form of a story, or am I just spewing a list of facts?

Talking to people *from* the heart and *to* the heart takes practice. It also takes extreme confidence and courage. For attorneys, it's probably not the daily mode of communication, but when coupled with the facts and the truth, it is the best mode of communication with the judge and jury.

Chapter 7:
Your Story: Building A Strong House

Your theme: the foundation of the house

"If the glove doesn't fit, you must acquit." Those words have made the history books. That was one of the *themes* with which Johnnie Cochran successfully represented O.J. Simpson. Cochran focused on this theme from the very beginning of the trial, even before he had that "tag line" to use with it. His theme always revolved around this one concept: yes, there's all this evidence to point to my client, but the evidence is wrong. It has been tainted, planted, and misinterpreted. *It doesn't fit my client.* When the glove did not seem to fit Simpson's hand, Cochran had a one-sentence "line" to sum up that theme and reinforce it over and over in the minds of the jury.

The theme of your case is not the "wherefores" and "hereinafters." It does not involve the legal jargon you may have used in the motions you filed with the court. It is short and sweet—there is no room for complicated legal terminology. Your theme is the essence, the heart, of your story. Preston Oade, a partner with Holme, Roberts & Owen in Denver, says it this way: "My theme answers every question that might come up in the case. No matter what question someone throws at me, a good theme will provide the answer."

For example, these simple themes answered every question in the cases in which they were used:

- It was not his idea.

- He was the one with all the choices.

- It all came down to the decisions she made.

When you are sure that you have come up with the perfect theme, write your opening. Then try to apply some of the elements of a great story to make the story more persuasive and less argumentative. Then rethink your theme. If it's the right one, you will have repeated it over and over again throughout the story. If you try to fit it in and it's like forcing a square peg into a round hole, then it's not the right theme for this case. The theme should reveal itself; it should be an easy fit. Many, many times, the perfect themes will not reveal themselves to you until a few days before the trial, when you are writing your opening statement.

The structure of the story: the frame of the house

Here's a tip that directors, screenwriters, and playwrights have known for years: what gets the most "air time" is what the audience focuses on. In the courtroom, whatever gets the most discussion in court is what the jurors spend the most time discussing in the jury room.

Gregory Cusimano and David Wenner, experienced trial lawyers, researched the implications of this theory a few years ago. What they discovered is something that runs counter to the way many trial lawyers have approached trials for decades, but that makes perfect sense when you think about how stories are structured by filmmakers and playwrights. It is best illustrated with an example. The following could be a typical opening statement told by a plaintiff's lawyer, and it is similar to this story told by Cusimano and Wenner in their research:

> Joe Smith was a great father and a kind and loving husband. He was the kind of man who put his family first. He had carefully structured his life in a way that allowed him quality time with his family. Joe was a successful architect, but he was determined not to let his work consume him. He arrived at work every day at 9:00, and left every day at 5:00, no matter how much work was still piled up on his desk. He was home by 5:30, cooked dinner with his wife, helped his kids with their homework, and read them a story at bedtime.
>
> One day—January 15th—Joe's wife was getting her wisdom teeth removed. The Smiths' neighbor was going to pick her up and take her home, but Joe wanted to be there when she got home, to take care of her, and to take care of the kids after school while she rested. So, on that day, he decided to leave at 2:00.
>
> At 2:00, Joe went out to the parking lot. As he got into his car, he realized, "Hey—I always take the same route home. Since I'm leaving before traffic, I can take the more scenic route, and it'll probably take me the same amount of time." So he took the scenic route.
>
> After ten minutes or so, Joe came to a light at the top of a hill. As he approached the intersection, the

light turned yellow. Joe was a careful driver, so he stopped at the light. He waited through the cycle, and when the light turned green again, he proceeded into the intersection. Halfway through the intersection, a drunk driver slammed into the side of Joe's car, killing him instantly. At Joe's funeral, all of his friends were saying, "Poor Joe. If only … ."

"If only" what? What would *you* say?

When we tell this story in our seminars, we hear answers like, "If only his wife didn't have her wisdom teeth out." "If only he hadn't stopped at the yellow light." "If only he had taken his usual route home." "If only he hadn't left early." "If only he had looked more carefully before he pulled out into the intersection."

On rare occasions, *one* person in the group might say, "If only the other driver wasn't drunk."

See the point? These questions aren't an attempt to "blame the victim." But the questions are looking for causation in the actions of the victim.

In the focus groups conducted by Cusimano and Wenner, 93 percent of the time, the answers centered around the actions of Joe Smith, not the drunk driver. It plays out the same way every time: people start dissecting the actions of the party you have just told them so much about. That's where you've focused the spotlight, so that's where they are going to look. They are going to look for ways to distance themselves from this victim, ways to try to persuade themselves that there is some semblance of control in life, that this victim somehow contributed to the accident.

For an attorney representing Joe Smith's family, there is a natural temptation to present Joe first: what a wonderful man he was, what his family has lost. But sympathy doesn't work, particularly in today's climate when jurors are wary of the motives behind lawsuits, playing the "sympathy card" will often backfire. Sympathy must be earned; it can't be elicited in one speech. Anger is much more powerful than sympathy. People hold onto it a lot longer and feel the need to do something about it. People are not called to action by sympathy: they are called to action by anger.

The best way to win for Joe Smith is to make the jurors angry at the defendant. To do that, you can almost take Joe out of the equation (until you're discussing damages). It's not *about* Joe Smith; it could have been anyone. It is about the actions of that drunk driver. It's about the choices *he* made. It's about *his* actions.

> It's 9:45 on January 15, and James Peters is already having a really bad day. He isn't feeling well, he's overslept, and he hit some heavy traffic on his way into work. He had a long night, though he doesn't remember a lot of it.
>
> When he gets to work, his co-workers are doing that thing people do when they are trying to politely avoid you. When they know something you don't.

James's boss calls him into his office around 10:15, and says, "James, I'm sorry. I've tried to work with you on this. I would still like to see you get some help. But this can't go on. You were late again this morning, you've been late six times in the past month, and I can't keep you here anymore. Please clean out your desk."

James has half an hour to clean out all of his stuff, and he is escorted from the building by security. His boss says it's company policy. Policy or not, it is humiliating.

James drives the four blocks to his friend's bar. He sits at the bar and has a sandwich and a scotch, and tells his friend about the rotten day he's having and the rotten way he's being treated. They discuss whether maybe he should sue the company for firing him. They talk about his girlfriend, Tanya. James was going to ask her to marry him, but this will probably set that back. They talk for three hours, and James drinks three more scotches, and two beers.

At 2:00, James decides he'd better head home and tell Tanya that he lost his job. As he gets into his car, he decides he should probably take the back roads—he feels fine, but since he's been drinking he doesn't want to risk another DUI, so he stays off the highway.

About ten minutes later, he comes up to an intersection, just as the light turns yellow. He thinks about stopping, but he doesn't. He goes through the red light, and slams into the side of a Buick in the middle of the intersection.

The driver of the Buick was Joe Smith, and Joe Smith was killed instantly when James Peters hit him. At Joe Smith's funeral, all of his friends were saying, "Poor Joe. If only … ."

Now what's your "if only"?

You may have noticed that we tried not to put any *judgment* into that story about James Peters. We tried to eliminate *argument* from the story—your opening statement is not the time for argument—you don't need it, and you don't have the credibility yet to get away with telling the jurors what to think. Just tell them the story, with all the details they need to see your painting, and shine the spotlight where you want them to look.

You want them to go into that jury room talking about the actions of the other party, not about the actions of your client. So make the story about the actions of the other party. Instead of saying, "My client called ABC Company and asked them repeatedly for a copy of his bill," try "ABC Company received repeated calls from my client, and they received repeated requests for a copy of his bill."

What if you're defending ABC Company? You certainly don't want to put any judgment into your story, but your story has to be about the plaintiff's actions. A lawyer came to us with a case where this might be a challenge. She said,

> My client, ABC Kitchen Design, did everything they were supposed to do for their customers. They did the same things that have made their customers happy for 25 years.
>
> They spent hours designing the perfect kitchen for their customer, Mr. King. They brought his dream kitchen to life on paper, and when they had gotten it just right, when Mr. King agreed that this was the perfect kitchen, they placed a large order for very up-scale cabinets on his behalf.
>
> Now, before ABC places an order like that, they always get a signed contract and a non-refundable deposit from their customer. On September 5th, Jennifer Smith, the design specialist who was working with Mr. King, explained this policy to him. She explained that the deposit, $10,000, was to cover design and materials and that it had to be received before any materials could be ordered. Ms. Smith received the signed agreement and the deposit from Mr. King on September 6.
>
> On September 7th, Ms. Smith placed the order for the cabinets, and prepared an order for the granite for the countertops. By this time, Ms. Smith had spent nine hours working on the design and ordering the materials for Mr. King's kitchen.

On September 17th, Ms. Smith called Mr. King to let him know that his cabinetry had been delivered. She left a message to that effect on his home voice-mail. On September 20th, when Ms. Smith hadn't heard from Mr. King, she called him again and left another message. She left numerous messages after that, with no response. Finally, on October 3rd, Ms. Smith received a call from Mr. King. He told her that he'd decided not to build the house, so he's not building his dream kitchen, and he wants his deposit back.

The ABC contract—which Mr. King signed—is very clear. It says really clearly that the deposit is *non-refundable*. But now the good people at ABC are being sued because of *his* mistakes.

She was telling us all about what her client had done—the time and money spent—and just devoted a few short sentences to the actions of the customer. We restructured the story this way:

Mr. King came into the ABC Kitchen Design on September 4th. He spent a few minutes looking at the cabinets and countertops on the showroom floor, then he asked to speak to a design specialist.

Mr. King had really done his research. He had a tote bag filled with kitchen design books and magazines. On a yellow legal pad, he had sketched out the kitchen of his dreams. He knew exactly what he wanted his new kitchen to look like.

When he sat down to talk with Jennifer Smith, the designer, she was impressed. Mr. King had researched the materials that would be best in this climate, he had measured every wall and angle, and he had a very clear idea of what he wanted to accomplish. He told her he was in the middle of building his dream house, and he wanted his dream kitchen to go into it. He asked for her suggestions about cabinetry, fixtures, appliances, and the accessories that you can build into kitchens these days—little baskets for dish towels or fruit, built-in cutting boards, things like that.

Mr. King talked with Ms. Smith for about two hours and left with a bag full of samples, swatches, and color cards, and an appointment to complete his design with Ms. Smith the next day.

The next day, on September 5th, Mr. King again sat down with Ms. Smith. He had made his decisions about cabinetry, countertops, and fixtures. Mr. King certainly knew his materials—he had chosen top-of-the-line products. He discussed some more design issues with Ms. Smith, made all his decisions, and signed off on a final design for his kitchen.

At this point, he asked Ms. Smith how soon she'd be placing the orders. She explained to him which vendors would be contacted for the products he had chosen. They discussed ABC's policy, which was to receive a non-refundable deposit before ordering any materials or products for a customer. Mr. King received the ABC contract, which clearly states the policy and the fact that the deposit is non-refundable. He told Ms. Smith he would return the next day with a check and the contract, once he'd looked it over.

The next day, September 6th, Mr. King delivered to Ms. Smith a deposit check for $10,000 and the signed contract. The next day, September 7th, Ms. Smith placed an order for the cabinets that Mr. King had picked out.

On September 17th, Ms. Smith called Mr. King to let him know that his cabinetry had been delivered. She left a message to that effect on his home voice-mail. Mr. King never returned her call. Between September 20th and October 3rd, Mr. King continued to ignore numerous voicemail messages from Ms. Smith. Finally, on October 3rd, Mr. King called back. He said that he'd decided not to build the house, so he wasn't going to build the kitchen, and he wanted his deposit back.

The ABC contract—which Mr. King signed—is very clear. It says really clearly that the deposit is *non-refundable*. But now he's suing to get the deposit back.

Any story can be structured to focus the spotlight on the actions of the other party, but you need the information to do it. You need enough details about the actions of the other party so that you can develop a compelling story that makes sense. This means you must start thinking this way before taking the depositions. You are going to need to get significantly more information than you think you could possibly need: information about what the deponents were doing the day before the incident in question, where they grew up, where they went to school, how they chose their career, how they chose the car they drive. You need this information because only then can you tell a complete story about *them.* And all of those details will enable you to show who these people are, what they did that the jurors should question, and what they did that the jurors should punish them for.

Take control of the picture, and shine the spotlight where it belongs: on the actions of the other party.

Another idea: parallel stories

There are many possible structures available to you. A great story is not always purely chronological. Think about how the previous story about Joe Smith and James Peters might be told in a movie:

> We open with a shot of Joe Smith pulling into the parking lot at his office. We see the clock on his dashboard: 9:00. He walks into the building, says "good morning" to people as he passes. He clearly has a good relationship with many people in his office. They like him. He stops to talk to Bob; they talk for a moment, and Joe tells him that he is

leaving early that day to take care of his wife after she has her wisdom teeth removed. Then Joe heads to his office. Cut to a clock on the wall: 9:15.

Cut to another clock on a bedside table. James Peters struggles awake, looks at the clock, jumps out of bed, cursing that he is late.

Cut to Joe's office: Joe is hard at work, discussing some blueprints with another architect.

Cut to James Peters, pulling fast into the parking lot at his office building. He jumps out of the car and rushes into the building. When he gets there, his co-workers look up, then quickly look away, avoiding his gaze. On James's way to his cubicle, a friend stops him and tells him the boss wants to see him right away. James goes to the boss's office, where the boss tells him that he's fired. The clock on the wall behind the boss says 10:30.

Cut to James, slamming his desk drawers as he is packing up his belongings. He grabs the box of his stuff and clutches it to his chest as he is escorted out of the building. He is obviously angry. Cut to clock above the door as he exits: 11:15.

Cut to a local bar. James pulls into the parking lot, clearly angry, the box from his desk on the seat next to him. He storms into the bar. He knows the bartender; they talk a bit, James complains about his boss firing him and expresses concern about how his girlfriend will take the news. He knocks back several drinks.

Cut to Joe Smith's office. Joe looks at a clock: 2:00. He packs his briefcase, says goodbye to some people in the office, and heads out to his car. He gets into his car.

Cut to James Peters at the bar. James tells the bartender he'd better get going, and break the news to his girlfriend. He walks outside, blinks in the sun, and gets into his car. The car clock says 2:00.

At this point, even if you haven't seen the previews, you know that James Peters is going to hit Joe Smith. The collision is inevitable. Through two parallel stories, the storyteller can lead the audience to jump to the conclusion ahead of time that the two stories are going to collide. The outcome seems inevitable.

"Availability bias"

Over 20 years ago, social scientists put a name to a phenomenon that influences the way we learn and process information. When we are learning something new, we develop a theory of *what happened.* Then we fill in any missing information using whatever information is available to us up to that point. That is called the "availability bias." If you have only told me about the plaintiff's actions and then I go looking to fill in a gap, I fill it with the behavior and actions of *the plaintiff,* because that is what is available to me.

A common gap that jurors try to fill is the question of "why" something happened. Motivation is very important. Have you ever heard a story that didn't ring true and asked something like, "Are you sure the teacher said that? Why in the world would he do that?" The lack of clear motivation makes the story less credible.

So, when listening to a story, we look for the "whys." And if the only information available to us is information about the behavior or decisions of your client, then that's where we'll look for that "why."

By showing us what happened, instead of just telling us, you can fill those gaps. Showing us how someone said something, rather than just telling us what she said, gives us information about her motivation and behavior. It gives us the information with which to support your theories.

The six elements of a great story: furnishing the house

Jurors are just like you and me. They all have lives outside the courtroom that they bring into the box everyday. They are thinking, "Will the kids get home safely from school?" "Will I have time to pick up the dry cleaning?" "Will my car get vandalized in the parking lot?" "Did I remember to feed the cat this morning?" To compete with these other "stories" floating around the courtroom, you must incorporate several key elements into *your* story.

A story has a "who," a "what," a "where," a "when," a "how," and, very importantly, a "why."

We have a very dear friend named Kevin. Kevin is a pretty thorough person—he does his research before he makes a major purchase. He decided to buy a new car and made a list of the features he wanted and the price range he was comfortable with. He narrowed it down to either Car A or Car B and went online to do his research. He looked at *Consumer Reports.* He looked at all of the car rating Web sites he could find. He read industry reviews, customer reviews, and looked up repair and consumer satisfaction ratings for those particular models.

After all of this research, he decided on Car A. He even researched dealers in his area and decided he was going to go to one of them the next day and buy Car A.

That night, he came to a dinner party at our house. He started talking to a mutual friend, Frank, about what he'd been doing lately, and the conversation came around to the car purchase. Frank said, "Oh, wow. You couldn't pay me to buy another [Car A]."

"Why?" Kevin asked.

"I had one for a few years, and it was a nightmare. First, when the car was only about six months old, the automatic window stopped working on the driver's side. It made this weird clicking noise for awhile, then it stopped altogether. It took them two weeks to fix that. Then it started to shimmy when

I braked going down a hill. That was another week in the shop, just to change the brake rotors. Then the car started making this weird noise from the back, like wind was going through a pipe. It wasn't very loud, but it was driving me nuts. I brought the car in *again,* and the dealership said, 'oh, don't worry about that. Some [Car A]s just do that in cold weather.' Well, I'm sorry, but that's not an acceptable answer! Finally, I just sold the darn thing."

Kevin didn't buy Car A.

Why? Why did one story over dinner trump all of Kevin's research, which showed that the odds were that it would be a great, reliable car for many years? Why did this story overcome all the evidence to the contrary?

For one thing, it was a personal story. This was a passionate account from someone who had personal experience. But that can't be all; what if Frank had just said, "Oh, wow. You couldn't pay me to buy another Car A. I had one for a few years, and it was a nightmare."

Would that have persuaded Kevin not to trust his research? Probably not. In addition to having detail, Frank's story was personal. The detail provided the credibility that caused Kevin to disregard his research. Frank had used two of the six elements of great storytelling—imagery and personal detail—to paint a clear and persuasive picture.

Element #1: Imagery and detail

It's all in the details. We experience, judge, and remember things through the use of our senses. Details make a story come alive. In a society infused with television and movie images, it is not enough to lay out simple facts. When we are listening to a story, we imagine the story happening. The more specifics the storyteller gives us, the more clearly (and correctly) we can visualize the event. If your story is easy for the jurors to visualize, it becomes a story they can relate to. By engaging their senses, you are engaging their minds, making them active, attentive participants who genuinely care about the outcome.

If you hear the words "executive office" what do you imagine? A big cherry-wood desk? A corner office with rich wood paneling? Dark leather furniture? We once had a client who was defending a case in which the plaintiff claimed to have had a meeting with a certain corporate executive in the executive's office. This meeting became an important factor in the case. We heard "executive" and "office," and everyone working on the case visualized a dark, elegant corner office. Finally, we asked our client, "What does this 'executive office' look like?" He didn't know, but he could find out. A few days later, our client called, elated. "It was a *cubicle!*" he laughed. That detail changed everything.

To make sure that jurors see the same picture you see, you must be specific. Use all five senses to show us what happened. Instead of just telling us what something looked like, tell us what it smelled like, or sounded like, or felt like. We experience the world through all five senses, and the more detail you can express, the more credible and persuasive your story becomes.

Be as specific as possible, and provide enough detail so that the jurors can't see the wrong picture. They may see the picture and decide they don't like it, but at least make sure they see the right picture!

Element #2: Personal involvement

Many attorneys seem to be afraid to express a passionate belief in their case in front of a jury—perhaps because they are trying to avoid looking insincere or melodramatic. While they are right that insincerity will destroy their credibility, they forget that a complete lack of passion for their case will do the same thing. Jury studies confirm that jurors want to see attorneys *advocate* for their client. It is not enough to be an objective voice in the courtroom; you are not there to offer objectivity. You are there because you believe in your client and you couldn't stay silent.

For you, the lawyer, to convince a modern jury that you are telling a true and important story and that your "ending" is the just ending, you must be personally involved in your story. If you seem to be an objective observer and even *you* don't really care, why should the jury? After all, if you really care about your client, you'll feel passionate about his or her story, right? And if you don't really care, then you must have taken the case just because of the money. If jurors believe that, then you have no credibility.

We've worked with many attorneys who are incredibly passionate about their client's cause when they are talking to us over coffee, but don't express that passion when delivering their opening statement. Your passionate belief in your cause is not only what makes jurors feel that your cause is just; it is also what keeps them actively listening to you, instead of thinking about their dry cleaning.

So, how do you let the jurors see that you are personally involved in your client's story? You *allow* yourself to express your belief in her cause, to argue passionately and with emotion. This does not mean you *act* emotionally. It simply means that you express your sincere belief in her cause. If you are having a hard time finding any empathy or emotion for a particular case or client, there are two simple exercises you can do during your preparation which will help you.

1. **Substitution.** Close your eyes, and imagine that what happened to your client happened instead to someone you love: a parent, a spouse, a child, maybe even yourself. Now rehearse your opening, keeping that image in the back of your mind. You're no longer talking about the CEO at Big Insurance Company; now you're talking about your daughter.

2. **Anchor sentence.** Find one passionate sentence that describes the injustice of what's happened to your client (e.g., "This is wrong!" or "This is ridiculous!"). Rehearse your opening, verbalizing that sentence after every few sentences of your argument. Then rehearse it again, without verbalizing your sentence, but keep thinking about that sentence.

Element #3: Story arc

The main difference between a story and a recitation of related facts is that a story has a beginning, a middle, and an end. Every good story has an "arc": the geometric form that exemplifies the changes that cause the story to move forward, and to end in a different place (physical, emotional, or otherwise) from where it begins.

Beginning ∎ *Middle* ∎ *End*

There are hundreds of possible beginnings to your story. Does it begin at the time of the accident? When the car was being designed? When the driver got into the car and didn't buckle her seatbelt? When the other driver ordered his third martini? Or even when your client woke up in the hospital bed with a tube down her throat?

The middle is a bit more defined, perhaps a few dozen possibilities. Think about where you want the jurors to go and how you can structure the middle of your story so that they get there before you do. It's always better if listeners are one step ahead of you by the time they reach the ending you're directing them to.

However, there can be only *one* ending to your story: a single, inevitable ending. And the jurors are going to write that ending for you. How well they write it depends in part on how well you have equipped them to write it—with information they can use to support your position. Have you given them the information they need? Have you filled in all the holes? Have you painted the picture so clearly that they see the same picture you see? Have you given them the *why*—the motivation of each character and the causation of each problem, so that they can judge the actions of the characters? Have you called them to action? Have you made their decision inevitable?

The "Vignette"—the smaller arc

Your story has sections, or chapters, that move the story forward. Each chapter has its own smaller arc—its own beginning, middle, and end. In each chapter something happens that changes the story and causes it to move in a new direction. Someone says something, does something—or specifically *doesn't* say or do something. We call these chapters "vignettes" because we want you to think of them as visual scenes in which an action takes place. By the end of each arc, there is a new element or an emotional change that causes the story to progress. In structuring your story, think about what these vignettes are and how you can make each one clear and engaging to your listeners so they understand how each arc moves the story forward.

Beginning ■ Middle ■ End—the bigger picture of the story arc

The beginning (opening statement)

One method of creating a clear picture of your client's story is to utilize the "whole–parts–whole' technique. The "whole–parts–whole' technique starts with presenting a complete overview of the story, from beginning to end, in a summary, as the "whole" story. Remember that this is the essence of your story and an overview of the facts that make up the story. This is your opportunity to engage your listeners in your theme—to give the jury a viewpoint from which to examine all the evidence presented throughout the trial.

The middle (presentation of evidence)

The middle deals with the details, or "parts," of the story, explaining each fact thoroughly and answering all questions. These are the facts that will be plugged into the story you told in your opening. They are the facts that make up the story, but they are not the story in and of themselves. Without the frame of reference established in your opening (in your story), they are just a list of facts.

The end (closing argument)

At the end of the story, a good storyteller returns to the "whole" story, completing the picture for the listener. This is your opportunity to review the way in which the facts relate to the story, how the facts support the story. But please remember, it is always the story that must be emphasized. Something *happened* to your client. If that something is effectively communicated to the jurors, the facts will already make sense to them in the context of your story. If not, the facts will be confusing or misleading—or worse, the jurors will fit the facts into your opponent's story.

Element #4: Present tense

By placing the story in the present tense, the story is happening now, and the listener is a part of it. Consider these two stories:

> Mike and Jane were driving down Main Street. They stopped at a light. A man stepped into the street and pointed a gun through the window at Jane.
>
> * * *
>
> Mike and Jane are driving slowly down Main Street. They stop for a red light. Suddenly, a man steps into the street and points a gun through the window at Jane.

The first story puts Mike and Jane inside a story that happened in the past. This story ended the night they were robbed. At this point, there's nothing the jurors can do about it. But the same story told in the present tense doesn't end until the jury *does something* to keep it from ever happening again. The jury can impact the story—make it right, right a wrong.

Aside from giving the jury the power to write *your* ending, putting a story in the present tense also creates a more vivid picture for the listener. If the story is happening *now*, a juror can't tune it out to make her grocery list. It also puts the audience on equal footing with the storyteller; they are experiencing it together. The story begins to exist again inside the walls of the courtroom. Every listener *envisions* the events, rather than simply thinking about them.

Element #5: Character development

Remember that when a case comes down to which party the jurors believe, they make their judgments about which party's story makes more sense by looking at the way each character makes decisions. If you are defending a manufacturer in a products liability case and the plaintiff claims that the product didn't operate properly, then you may need to show us how the plaintiff makes decisions: whether she asks for help, works too fast, tries to accomplish more than any of the other workers, attempts difficult tasks on her own, etc. By showing us how she makes decisions, you show us who she is and we gain insight into how she might have gotten herself into this situation in the first place.

It is not necessary to attack the other party to use character development to show that your case is the just one. In fact, it is almost always more effective *not* to attack. Simply show the jurors what the other party did in various situations—how he made various decisions in life—and let the jurors come to the conclusion that the character of this person is not consistent with his claims.

For example, we had a client who was defending a broker in a securities fraud case. The plaintiff wanted the jurors to see her as a victim: an elderly widow who was not in a position to control her accounts. Our client knew that in reality she was a sophisticated, strong woman who had extensive investment experience and made all the decisions regarding her accounts. During her opening statement, our client briefly recounted the plaintiff's life story, showing a woman who was strong enough to get married against her parents' wishes, build a successful career in a "man's occupation," and handle her husband's affairs after his death. The picture was clear: this was a woman who was in control of her life. She made the decisions. The argument that she had been uninvolved in the decisions made about her brokerage accounts didn't make sense once the jurors had that picture of her character.

Element #6: Genuine drama

It is vitally important to allow the listener to experience the genuine drama of your client's story. Many attorneys stay away from the drama of the story in an effort to stay away from melodrama. They are right: melodrama has no place in a courtroom. However, drama is inherent in every case that makes it to trial. The stakes are huge. By allowing the jury to experience the drama, you allow them to make an emotional investment in the outcome.

The difference between drama and melodrama is simple: drama is real, melodrama is not. For example, an attorney's client is walking down the street and suddenly he finds himself surrounded by a gang of thugs. The gang is looking at him like they want to rob and kill him. What does the trapped man do? Does he run? Does he fight? No matter what he does, that is a dramatic situation.

Melodrama, on the other hand, is not real. Most of the time, it is created in the mind rather than the actual event. For example, the man is walking down the street and sees some kids on the other side of the street just minding their own business, but the man *imagines* that these kids could be dangerous and creates in his mind this whole scenario of what *might* happen, even though nothing real has happened at all. This person has created a melodrama.

Melodrama is the style of acting that we associate with a silent film. Everything is exaggerated: the back of the grief-stricken maiden's hand pressed against her forehead with a sigh. Melodrama can be very entertaining, but it is not sincere. It has its place perhaps, but not in the courtroom. Anything that is insincere damages the attorney's credibility with the jury.

But that does not mean that an advocate should not be passionate, animated, and *dramatic*. To understand *drama*, compare the style of melodrama with the acting style of Robert DeNiro or Meryl Streep. "Realistic" actors like this strive to honestly convey the *real* emotions experienced by their characters. So should it be with litigators: the advocate must convey to the trier of fact the *sincere* and very *real* pain suffered by her client. She must speak honestly and passionately about the injustice that has been, or is being, done to that client. She must allow the *real drama* into the courtroom.

In the courtroom, melodrama will result in a loss of credibility with the jury, while genuine drama will bring them to tears or anger, and call them to action.

Chapter 8:
How To Rehearse Your Story

It is essential to rehearse your story aloud. No matter how many times you run something over in your head—making sure every nuance, every intonation, every inflection is perfect—it will sound completely different the first time you say it aloud. At acting auditions, the waiting room is full of grown men and women wandering around, talking to themselves. Actors have learned, through many tongue-tied moments, the importance of letting the mouth get as used to our lines as the brain is. An amazing bonus is that if we have rehearsed aloud *several times*, our mouth will remember the words even when our brain is taking a lunch break.

Rehearsing aloud is especially important when it comes to asking for what you want. If you get tongue-tied while asking the jury to award your client $300,000, you can bet they will doubt whether even *you* think that is a fair figure.

If confidentiality permits, rehearse your story with someone other than an attorney. If you have children, tell them a bed-time story and notice the simplicity of it. Observe what captivates the child and how "caught up in the story" she becomes. This is how the jury must understand your story, not as a fairy tale, but in clear and real terms. Does the story make sense to you? Not in the legal sense, but just as information that is understandable?

Exercises

1. **Tell your story to a child.** This is not a commentary on the mentality of jurors, but on the complexity of legalese. If a child can understand and stay interested in your story, you have gotten it down to the basics. Any subtleties you add now are a bonus, as long as they don't cloud the story with unnecessary terminology or confusing tangents.

2. **Yell your story.** Remember to be careful not to strain your voice. Breathe correctly. Make it as loud as you can, but not to the point where you are straining or screaming. This exercise will help you engage your body in the story, as well as helping you to eliminate some of the extraneous legal language that you might otherwise overlook.

3. **Whisper your story.** As loudly as you can (again, without straining), tell your story as if you were whispering it to someone across the room.

4. **Tell your story without your voice.** We first discussed this method in Chapter 4. Tell someone your story using nothing but physical gestures. When you finish, have your listener speak the story back to you as he or she understood it. You then fill in any missing pieces of important information, again using only gestures. This exercise will lead you directly to the heart of your case; you will find the most important moments, the essence of your story, and how the facts fit into that story.

5. **Get comfortable.** How would you tell this story if, instead of standing nervously in a courtroom, you were sitting comfortably on your couch? Try it. Feel the difference in your "presentation" when you are completely comfortable. Halfway through your story, stand up and maintain that feeling.

The preceding exercises are designed to engage your entire body in the telling of your story and to help you break old patterns. Any time you feel yourself turning into *Lawyer Man*, practicing these techniques will help you get back to the essence of your story. They also inspire a new vision of your presentation and release the creativity we all tend to bury under layers of social training. You'll be amazed at what you'll learn. Most of all, you'll learn to *let go*.

Storytelling Worksheet

[**Note:** An electronic copy of this worksheet is included on the CD-ROM in the "Worksheets" folder.]

1. Tell your story in six sentences. Make sure your story has a beginning, a middle, and an end.

   _____

   _____

2. Whom do you want the trier of fact to focus on during deliberations? How will you shine the spotlight on his or her actions when you compose your story?

   _____

   _____

3. What is the *beginning* of your story?

   _____

   _____

4. What is the *ending* of your story?

   _____

   _____

5. What are your key *themes*? Remember: your theme should be a very brief sentence that answers every question in the case. It should fit on a bumper sticker.

   _____

   _____

6. How are you going to *show* the jurors what happened, instead of *telling* them? What gestures will you use to illustrate the picture?

---

7. List any part of your story in which you relate something that someone *said*. How will you take control of the picture and present what they said to *show* the trier of fact the context, attitude, and the like?

---

8. Story Arc: List the "vignettes" or "chapters" of your story (not of your *opening statement,* but of the *story* of what happened to your client.)

---

9. Personal Involvement: Do you feel passionate about your client's cause? If not, practice one of the exercises listed in this section to increase your personal stake in the story. Write down what thoughts, memories, and so on succeed in making you feel more strongly for your client.

---

10. Character Development: Who are your main characters in this story? List them, and write at least three words to describe each of them.

_____

_____

11. Drama: What is the *drama* of your story?

_____

_____

12. Imagery and Detail: List at least ten words in your opening statement that evoke powerful imagery.

_____

_____

13. Rehearse your story using only gestures—no words. Try to convey as much detail as possible. What did you learn? What gestures will you incorporate into your opening? Did you learn new information about your case or your characters?

_____

_____

14. Rehearse your story aloud, incorporating the work you've already done in these worksheets. What did you learn? What worked, and what didn't? What needs changing? What needs clarification?

_____

_____

15. Rehearse your story for a non-attorney. What questions did he or she ask? What moments did you clarify? What did you learn about your story?

_____

_____

16. List the most technical or complicated facts/testimony you will be presenting during the trial. How do these facts fit into your *story?* What *analogy* will you use to make those facts clear to a jury?

_____

_____

17. Notes and observations:

_____

_____

Chapter 9:
The Credibility Factor

James McElhaney suggests that underlying every trial is a simple progression:

I am honest.

You should believe me.

I believe in the justice of my client's cause.

Therefore, you should decide for my client.

McElhaney suggests that credibility is the single most important gauge for everything you do. "How will this affect my credibility as an advocate?" is a good vantage point for examining everything you do in the course of a trial. If you intend to do something that might harm your credibility, don't do it.

The most simple case, the most stunning argument, the most intriguing story—all mean nothing if the jury doesn't believe you.

Aside from your voice, eye contact, and body language, there are a few things you may not think about that can affect your credibility in the courtroom:

1. **Telling the Truth.** It may sound obvious, but "fudging the truth" or ignoring facts that you feel damage your case can cause more harm than good. If you have a

hole or weakness in your case and you tell the jury about it yourself, you maintain your credibility. If you are credible and jurors believe you, then they are more likely to accept your explanation of that hole or weakness. The most damaging result of not admitting your weaknesses is not the fact that you are forced on the defensive when opposing counsel brings it up; it is the loss of your credibility in the eyes of the jury.

2. **Listening.** If you don't hear or if you ignore an answer to your questions (whether in voir dire or examination), you damage your credibility. Suddenly, you embody all those terrible lawyer jokes. When a "real person" is engaged in conversation, what he or she says comes naturally out of what the other person says. A good listener reacts to what the other person says and does. If you operate from a list of questions, without responding as a "real person" to what is really being said, you lose the respect and trust of the jury.

3. **Reading your argument.** If you are reading *facts* to the jury, they will correctly assume that you are being careful, making sure you get the facts straight. But if you have to read your notes to *explain* those facts to them, it looks as thought you don't know what you are talking about—or worse, that you don't believe your own argument. For this reason, we recommend using a speaking outline. Now, there is an exception to this rule. We have a client who is an exceptional trial lawyer. He conducts extensive jury research on his high-stakes cases, and from that research, he and his

consultants write a beautiful opening statement. He swears by these opening statements and notes that he would rather have an associate read them than blunder through a poor version without reading it. There is a good point to be made here: you must tell your client's story; you must get the facts out there. If you are not able to do that without reading your opening statement, then you may be *forced* to read it to the jury. But if you put down the file and invest in some extra time practicing your opening statement aloud, we think you will find you are more than capable of presenting a compelling, persuasive, and credible argument with the use of an outline instead of a script.

The Credibility Factor
Worksheet

[**Note:** An electronic copy of this worksheet is included on the CD-ROM in the "Worksheets" folder.]

1. List any "problems" you perceive in your case and the way you will present these problems to the jury.

   _____

   _____

2. List any aspects of your *case* that might possibly damage your credibility. How will your present these aspects to prevent such damage?

   _____

   _____

3. List any aspects of your *presentation,* or that of your witnesses, that might possibly damage your credibility. Also list solutions to the problems.

   _____

   _____

Chapter 10:
Stage Presence:
It's All In The Listening!

"To speak is to sow; to listen is to reap."

— Turkish Proverb

If you want the jury to believe that you are their own representative in the courtroom, that your story is the one that they should believe, you must be more *present* than anyone else in the courtroom.

Stage presence is exactly that: *presence* in the room. If you are thinking about your next question while the last question is being answered, how *present* are you? If you don't hear a joke being made because you are taking notes, are you really *present* in the courtroom? The only way to be genuinely present in the room, and therefore to have "stage presence," is to *actively listen* to what is going on around you.

Presence is not something you must be born with. It is not some mysterious gift reserved for the naturally talented. Presence can be learned, practiced, and cultivated. Have you ever noticed that Robert DeNiro very rarely does interviews? Watching him on screen, he has enormous "stage presence," doesn't he? All eyes look to him, the camera "loves" him, you just can't stop watching him. Yet in person, he could be in the same room with you for an hour and you wouldn't even know that he was there. His "presence" comes not from being some kind of larger-than-life superhuman. It comes from his awareness that to be a great actor, one must be a great listener. It comes from his ability to turn silence into action, suspense—into communication in itself.

Listening during the silence

You must be present, connected to the jurors and the others in the room, and listening to what's going on, even when nothing is being said. Sometimes, the greatest moments happen in the silence. Amateurs think that silent pauses make them look dumb. Professionals know they make them look smart.

We all have a natural desire to fill the silence. If the audience seems restless or uninterested, the amateur actor will speed up, trying to fill all the silent moments in an attempt to make what is happening on stage more "interesting." The professional actor, in the same situation, will *slow down*, knowing that *suspense* comes out of silence. Many advocates feel self-consciousness with silence and keep talking to fill it. Realize that if you remain *present*, by listening to and being aware of your environment, then your "audience" will be intrigued during silence, not bored by it. Have you ever fallen asleep with the television or radio on? If someone turns *off* the television or radio, what happens? You wake up. Sometimes, a moment of silence can be just the change in pattern that "wakes up" your listeners. Let the pause swell. Let the silence create suspense in your listeners.

Actors use the silence to stay present. Actors learn that truly great acting usually comes in *reacting*. Have you ever seen an amateur actor who seems very involved in speaking his lines, but seems totally uninvolved when he is *not* speaking? You, as the audience, cannot possibly believe this actor if he doesn't appear to be *hearing* what the other characters are saying to him. If you can't *listen*, why should the jurors believe you?

Some of the most dramatic and compelling human reactions occur when someone is listening and reacting honestly to what is happening to them, not when they are speaking. In the film *Dominic and Eugene,* the most dramatic scene is a two-minute close-up of Tom Hulce, when his character realizes what happened to him as a child. There is no dialogue, no music, nothing but his human, open, and brutally honest reaction. In *My Cousin Vinny,* watch Marissa Tomei in the climactic scene where she is on the stand. When she realizes where Joe Pesci is going with his questions, Pesci is speaking but the camera is on *her.* She is listening, and her *reaction* is the drama.

Another great example can be seen in the film *Glengarry Glen Ross.* Jack Lemmon plays an over-the-hill salesman who is desperate to make a big sale to save his career. In one scene, he is jubilant, because he believes he's just closed the deal. Kevin Spacey, playing his boss, tells Lemmon that the buyers he thinks he's made the sale to have been doing this for months—they commit to a salesman but don't have any money. There is no sale. Through the camera lens, we watch Jack Lemmon hear and process this information. We see him come crashing down, without hearing him say a word.

Half of acting is RE-acting, and to react you must listen

You must truly care about and hear the words spoken and the answers given, but you must also allow yourself to respond to the non-verbal cues of your listeners and the activity going on around you. In any conversation, human beings respond to each other and to outside stimuli. If a car alarm goes off, or a microphone squeals, or you knock over your water glass, you must acknowledge it to maintain your credibility.

On stage, if an actor spills something, the audience will stop listening to the dialogue and fixate on the spill until someone cleans it up. An actor can't pretend that it's not there, or that he or she does not see or hear something everyone else sees or hears. If the jury hears the door slam or the court reporter coughing uncontrollably, and you *don't* hear or respond to them as a human being would, you further distance yourself from the jurors. You tell them that you're nervous or that you just don't care enough to pay attention to what's going on around you. Ultimately, not responding to the stimuli in your environment damages your credibility with the jury.

Active listening doesn't mean just listening to what is being said. It means becoming the most interested person in the courtroom, not the most *interesting*. It means paying attention to what is *not said*. It is hard, exhausting work, but it is invaluable.

The art of listening

What is the audience's role in your presentation?

We often tell our clients to "have a conversation with the jury." To which they often reply, "How can I have a conversation when they can't speak back to me?" For an actor, "listening" means being willing to be changed by what is going on around him. Are you willing to change your opening based on what you hear from opposing counsel in her opening or voir dire? Are you willing to skip some of your questions during voir dire because you are having a valuable conversation with the jurors? Are you willing to repeat or rephrase part of your closing argument because you see that a number of jurors look confused?

Awareness of the audience is something that the theater professional is quite familiar with. Len tells this story:

> I had a remarkable experience once, while on stage in Anton Chekhov's *The Cherry Orchard.* It was clear from the first scene of the play that the audience was really into the show and having a great time. They were laughing and, quite clearly, they were paying very close attention to what was happening on stage. I remember being on stage and suddenly feeling intimidated, as if there was something wrong with my performance. It was only when I started to relax and play off of the audience that I truly felt the sensation of having a conversation with them. Wow, what an incredible feeling!

What we mean by "playing off of the audience" is allowing yourself to pause and listen to their reactions, and to accept and encourage their enthusiasm, rather than having Len's initial reaction, which was to feel intimidated and, quite frankly, a bit shocked.

Often, attorneys become so wrapped up in the fine points of their courtroom presentations that they forget to take the time to look and listen. The conversation that we are speaking of is an exchange of energy and ideas through non-verbal communication, such as eye contact, body language, and facial expression.

Here is another example:

> I was sitting on an airplane and noticed a young boy struggling to reach a pillow in the overhead bin above his seat. There he was making little jumps on the seat cushion, never quite getting his hand on that elusive pillow. I glanced over to my left, and the man sitting across the aisle had an amused grin on his face as he watched our determined young neighbor struggling for his pillow. The boy finally snared the pillow, and I shared a glance with my row mate. We smiled at each other, chuckled a bit to ourselves, and then went on with what we were doing. We had a shared moment together, for just a few seconds. Those same moments can happen during your opening statement if you will just take the time to look, and listen to the trier of fact.

Let's take an example from an actual case:

> We were practicing an opening statement with a lawyer who was having difficulty getting "out of her

head"—in other words, it was as if she were reciting a memorized script and having a hard time remembering her lines. Clearly, she was not able to listen to the jury.

Through practice and a bit of coaching, she was finally able to relax enough and to trust that she would know what to say to the jury, rather than trying to recite a memorized presentation. She paused, connected with a juror, and said, "The evidence is clear that the plaintiff knew the dangers involved in using my client's product, and knew the precautions he should have been taking." Then, she paused, and looked at each person, nodding to them, and they nodded back in agreement. She took the time to look, listen and connect, and hence, brought the level of communication between her and the jury to a deeper and more personal level.

How to become an expert listener

Listening is a skill; very few people do it naturally. For most of us, it requires practice. The good news is that just for practicing this skill, you will receive countless rewards, both professionally and personally. Practice *actively listening*, without thinking about what you are going to say next. As Stephen Covey suggests in *The Seven Habits of Highly Effective People*, seek first to understand, *then* to be understood. Practice with your colleagues; you'll be amazed at how "interesting" and "intelligent" you suddenly become to them. Really listening is harder than you'd think, and few people make the effort. Most people take conversation for granted and are not used to truly being *heard*. You'll notice the gratitude of others when you actively listen to them.

Presence & Spontaneity
Worksheet

[**Note:** An electronic copy of this worksheet is included on the CD-ROM in the "Worksheets" folder.]

1. Are you allowing moments of silence, or speaking just to fill them? List at least one moment in your opening statement when it would be most effective to let a silent pause swell.

   _____

   _____

2. List at least one moment where you can use silence to your advantage in:

   Voir Dire _____

   _____

   Opening/Closing _____

   _____

   Cross-Examination _____

   _____

   Direct _____

   _____

3. Notes and observations:

   _____

   _____

Chapter 11:
Relationships

The actor knows that what the audience responds to are his relationships with the other characters. Drama comes from interplay between people. Your willingness to engage in human relationships—with the witnesses, with your client, with the jury—is what will encourage the jurors to care about you, and therefore your client. No matter how technical or boring the testimony, if you are actively engaged in a relationship with the witness, the jury will be compelled to watch and seek to understand. The relationships being played out in the courtroom are the most interesting thing for the jury to watch.

Your relationship with your client

Your relationship with your client is what tells the jury that you believe in your client, that he or she is credible. Allow yourself to relate to your client in front of the jury as you would relate to a friend. They will sense the implication that you trust and believe in your client. James McElhaney recommends rehearsing your relationship with your client, and with your witnesses, just as you would rehearse important testimony. This does not mean that you must "plot" a pat on the back or a hand on your client's shoulder. It simply means that you discuss your relationship with your client and—assuming you truly do *like* and *believe* this person—allow that relationship to be seen by the jury. The audience will perceive your relationships in the courtroom, whether good or bad, so this rehearsal can help you to consciously affect those perceptions.

Creating a positive relationship

Clark Gable had notoriously bad breath. Montgomery Clift was rumored to be emotionally unstable. Yet the actresses playing opposite these stars were required to gaze lovingly at them, passionately kiss them, and convince the audience that they were the sexiest and most desirable men in the world.

Similarly you, as the advocate, must be able to show the jury positive feelings about a person towards whom you may not have any positive feelings. You must be able to interact with people in a way that exhibits the most effective relationship. You must be able to show respect for a judge whom you believe to be inept, or appear confident before a judge who intimidates you. You must be able to convey trust and belief in a client who is unreliable or unsympathetic. You must express your confidence in witnesses who concern you with their unpredictability. You must express your unshakable self-confidence in your interactions with an intimidating opposing counsel.

One technique that actors use when forced to express positive feelings about a despicable character is called *role playing.* Imagine the person you are interacting with as a *different* person who inspires the qualities you wish to convey. For instance, if you are intimidated by the opposing counsel, take a moment to imagine her as the woman who works at your gym or your cousin—any person who does not intimidate you. Everyone has heard the suggestion that we "imagine that the people who intimidate us are in their underwear," but sometimes we need to elicit a response in ourselves other than laughter. If you are cross-examining a belligerent witness and find yourself getting annoyed, imagine that he is your cantankerous uncle or a fussy child—someone who inspires patience instead of anger.

If your client makes you feel frustrated instead of sympathetic, imagine someone you care about in the same circumstances. For instance, if you are defending a sexual harassment suit and you are having a hard time feeling righteous indignation for your client, imagine that your father, husband, or brother were standing accused of these horrible things. Spend a few minutes visualizing this. What impact does it have on your family? What does it make you feel?

Find a way to change your perceptions, even momentarily, to allow you to interact with the other people involved in the trial in a way that shows you, your case, and your client in the best possible light.

Your relationship with yourself: talking to yourself

How many times have you heard the phrase, "Be nice to yourself" or "You're too hard on yourself"? It's part of being human that often times we expect far more from ourselves than we would ever dream of expecting from other people. In communication, however, how we speak with ourselves is critical to how we communicate with others. When faced with the reflection of our listener, we will often see a true picture of ourselves.

So the first step in mastering the art of communication is talking to and with yourself. Ask yourself, "What exactly am I saying in my mind before I walk into the courtroom?" Before I walk into a deposition? Before a settlement conference? Before speaking with the judge? Before opening statements? Before direct examination? Before cross-examination? We all engage in a kind of inner dialogue or "self-talk" as we approach these tasks, often without even being aware of it.

Walking into the courtroom

> *This is so messed up! I didn't sleep well last night, and I can't believe that they can get away with charging $15 a day for parking! Okay, okay, let's get focused here. Where's my client? No problem, he'll be here on time. He better be here on time! Jeez, my back is killing me again. Whatever. Okay, focus, focus, focus. Let's go over these motions again. Judge Jones can be such an idiot when it comes to these things!*

Do these kinds of thoughts run through your mind on your way to court? Perhaps you're thinking, "Yeah, so what? Just another average day!" However, this kind of *negative* self-talk does nothing to prepare your mindset for succeeding in the *task at hand.* The key to speaking to yourself is focusing on the task at hand.

Say, for example, that the task at hand is arguing a summary judgment motion. All the other issues that have affected your day are irrelevant to the task at hand. What if your inner dialogue went something like this:

> "Okay, the first 30 seconds when I'm talking are critical. What am I going to say or do to keep the judge's attention?"

Or:

> "I like the last statement on page 11 in paragraph 2. The long pause I added after the statement really emphasizes ... ."

Or:

> "Focus on the people in the room. Be externally focused. Focus on the judge receiving the information."

This kind of *positive* self-talk constructively helps you prepare for the task at hand.

Relationships
Worksheet

[**Note:** An electronic copy of this worksheet is included on the CD-ROM in the "Worksheets" folder.]

1. Describe your relationship with your client. Is it as positive as it can be? How can you express its most positive qualities to the jury?

    _____

    _____

2. List at least six qualities you admire about your client.

    _____

    _____

3. Describe your relationship with each of your key witnesses.

    _____

    _____

4. What is your relationship with the judge? Is it positive? If so, how will you express that to the jury? If not, how can you make it *appear* positive?

    _____

    _____

Notes and observations:

    _____

    _____

Part 3.

Putting It All Together For Trial

"What is true is what I can't help believing."

— Oliver Wendell Holmes, Jr.

"True does not mean factual (though it may be factual); true means accurately reflecting human experience... In the presence of a true story, we say, 'Yes, this is how it feels; this is how it would happen; this is what one might think.'"

— Daniel Taylor

"The truth is more important than the facts."

— Frank Lloyd Wright

"A story must be judged according to whether it makes sense. And "making sense" must... be understood in its most direct meaning: to make sense is to enliven the senses."

— David Abram

"A jury consists of twelve persons chosen to decide who has the better lawyer."

— Robert Frost

Chapter 12:
Preparing Yourself And Your Witnesses
For Depositions And Trial

The deposition you're taking

Many depositions are taken out of habit—without much thought about the goals for the deposition. Before you notice a deposition, determine your goals. Are you taking the deposition to contain a witness to his position? To preserve his testimony for trial? To strengthen your motion to dismiss? For discovery? Maybe you have multiple goals for the deposition? James McElhaney, in *Trial Notebook*, discusses some of these goals in detail. For our purposes, we're going to discuss the best ways to get important story information in a deposition.

Getting information that is useful for your story

This leads us back to our section on the power of story-telling (Part 2 of this book). You should already have an idea of the story you want to tell. To put the focus on the actions of the other party (see Chapter 7), you'll need more detailed information than you might ordinarily get in a deposition. Make sure to define your goals before you walk into the room. You are not just there to gather information, you are *looking* for specific information that can confirm and add credibility to the story you need to tell. Obviously, what you learn might change the story you decide to tell, but think in terms of getting thorough details, enough to build a story about the actions of the other party.

What information are you looking for in order to flesh out the story that you have decided to explore? What vignettes are undeveloped or need further clarification? (See Chapter 7.) Your story has sections, or chapters, that move the story forward. Each chapter has its own smaller arc—its own beginning, middle, and end. In each chapter, something happens that changes the story and causes it to move in a new direction. Someone says something, does something—or specifically *doesn't* say or do something. We call these chapters "vignettes" because we want you to think of them as visual scenes in which an action takes place. By the end of each arc, there is a new element or an emotional change that causes the story to progress. In planning to take a deposition, think about what these vignettes are and what information you'll need to make each one clear and engaging to your listeners.

How does the witness fit into the story or this particular vignette? What can you discover about your own client's perceived role in these vignettes?

Remember, you want to *show* the jurors what happened, instead of telling them what happened (Chapter 6). In order to do that, you'll need more details than just the words that were used. In addition to asking a witness *what* was said in a conversation, also ask her *how* it was said. You could tell the jury, "at that time, Nancy Jones threatened her employer, Mr. Miller."

But when you are telling the jury about a conversation, it is more persuasive and more credible to say, "Nancy Jones stormed into the room and said, 'you aren't going to get away with treating me this way.'" In a deposition, if a witness is telling you about a conversation, ask her to "act out" the conversation for you—show you exactly what was said and how it was said.

If you're going to show the jury what happened, and lead them to a particular conclusion, a detailed story is the only way to do it. Details are essential to any compelling and credible story. For instance, in a car accident case, it's more effective to *show* the jury that the plaintiff was driving irresponsibly than to simply tell the jury "Ms. Williams was speeding." Further, you may suspect that the plaintiff was speeding, but not have evidence to back up that suspicion. Asking in deposition, "how fast were you going?" will most likely not result in the answer you're hoping for. Get the information you need more indirectly. While you're asking her about her work, also ask where her office is, and how far it is from her home, what time she starts work. Note: if you can make this whole line of questioning feel like you're just chatting—as you would at a dinner party— you'll stand more chance of getting accurate, unguarded responses. For instance, rather than looking at your pad, looking up, and asking, "what time are you expected to start work every day?" you might get more information if you ask, "what's your boss like? Can you get in whenever you want to in the morning, or is she pretty strict?" Later in the deposition, while discussing the day of the accident, ask what time she left for work. At another time during the deposition, find out how far the accident site is from her home. You may then be able to put together a story that persuades the jury that she was rushing, late for work, and probably wasn't paying enough attention to the road.

"Ms. Williams left her home every morning at 8:30, to be at work at 9:00. Her office is at the corner of Main and Elm Street, about 23 miles from her home. That commute is mostly on the highway, so leaving thirty minutes before she has to be at work gets her to the office with enough time to park and walk into the building. This is important for her, because her boss is very strict about starting work on time. Her boss actually called Ms. Williams into her office the week before the accident, to tell her how important it was to be on time. On the morning of the accident, Ms. Williams received a call from her mother at 8:15. Her mother wanted to tell her some important news about Ms. Williams' sister, who was going through a divorce. By the time the call ended, it was 8:35. Ms. Williams bundled up, and went outside to start the car and scrape the ice from the windshield. She pulled out her driveway sometime between 8:40 and 8:45. At 9:05, the time of the accident, Ms. Williams was at the corner of James Street and Maple."

Now you won't have to tell them that Ms. Williams was in a hurry. They already have that picture.

How to get more detailed answers

Obviously, open-ended questions will elicit more detailed responses than yes/no questions. Remember, this is not cross-examination. That trial advocacy "rule" about never asking a question to which you do not know the answer *cannot* apply to a deposition. You need to get the answers here. If you start from the beginning, encouraging the witness to give you long, detailed responses, you'll get longer answers when you get to the "meaty" questions as well. So, instead of asking "When did you move to Colorado?", ask "Tell me about what brought you to Colorado?" Get the witness into the habit of giving you long, detailed, complete narratives right from the start.

Remember, most people don't like silence and tend to try to fill it (see Chapter 10). If you don't fill the silence, the witness will, so you can use this tendency to encourage a more detailed response. If you do this effectively, the witness will begin to ramble, and many times that is when the gems appear. To do this effectively involves more than just not speaking. If the witness answers your question and you do not jump right into the next question, but you look down at your notes or otherwise break contact with him, you are taking the responsibility for the conversation onto yourself, and the witness will not feel obligated to fill the silence. If you continue to look at him, and continue to place the burden of the conversation upon *him*, he will feel the need to fill the silence you have created. This can be as simple as maintaining eye contact with him and looking to him for the rest of the answer that you know is there. If you do this effectively, he will reward you with more information than you could have hoped for, while his attorney beats her head against the proverbial wall. Remember to prepare *your* witnesses to expect this technique from opposing counsel as well (see "Preparing witnesses for deposition," page 165 below).

Important tips

1. **Active listening is essential.** Everyone knows that listening is important. If you aren't listening, you'll miss important follow-up opportunities. "Active listening" is a bit more specific. It means actively listening to every word that comes out of the witness' mouth, and analyzing what you hear. It means never thinking about your next question, or taking notes while the witness is speaking. This type of listening will elicit more detailed answers, and ensure that you don't miss a golden opportunity.

2. **Make sure you get the sound bites.** If you are looking for specific information, make sure you get it in a form that will sound good if played in court. If the answer is good for you, but it is unclear, imprecise, or ambiguous, then it won't make the impact you need in the courtroom. Narrow the witness down to the sound bite.

3. **Do your homework.** Prepare, prepare, prepare. An excellent attorney we work with schedules two full prep days for every scheduled day of deposition. If you've done your homework, you'll know which comments open doors to new information. You'll know where the lies are, where the truth is being manipulated, where the missteps are. If the witness—as well as opposing counsel—knows that you're prepared, you'll get more accurate information, and maybe improve your chances of settlement. But beware: showing off your knowledge is a poor goal in and of itself. Remove your ego from the process.

4. **Don't ask one question too many.** In the car accident example above, don't ask the follow-up question, "so you were in a hurry?" Don't give her the opportunity to say, "No. I decided it was more important to drive safely than to get to work on time. Ironic, don't you think?"

5. **Don't forget the "why" questions.** Many depositions have the "who," "what," and "where" questions, but are missing the "why" questions. Why did Ms. Smith leave late that morning? Why did she move from New Jersey to Illinois?

6. **Test various forms of questioning with key witnesses.** What makes the witness angry? What makes him sad? What makes him lose his temper? How strong is his resolve? What makes him stand firm?

7. **Create an outline to get the story:**

   a. You have to know what you *think* your story is going to be, and be flexible enough to change it if the information you're getting is leading in a different direction.

   b. Identify the possible vignettes, or chapters, of your story (see Chapter 7) and create an outline of the story, with each vignette listed. Use a best-case scenario: if you had vignettes to back up the best story you can think of, what would they be?

   c. Formulate questions designed to flesh out each of the vignettes. Remember that each vignette has a beginning, a middle, and an end.

d. Identify the information that is missing from each vignette, and add blank bullet points to that part of your outline. Now you know where the holes are.

The deposition you're defending

Video depositions

Recently, a client shared a video deposition horror story:

> "My partner defended a deposition for me once, and the deposition was taken on video. When he got back to the office, he told me the deposition had gone fairly well. I popped in the tape, and up popped my witness, with a very large Bird of Paradise growing out of the top of her head. My partner had sat next to her, and had not checked to see what she looked like through the camera lens. The deposition was taken in a conference room, and directly behind her was a Bird of Paradise plant. Since then, I always take a look through the lens, to make sure my witness looks good."

This story teaches a valuable lesson. We've seen video depositions in which the witness is framed, lit, or placed in the room in such a way that she looks shifty, silly, or dishonest. Sometimes it is purely a result of ignorance on everyone's part. But sometimes we feel it could have been intentional on the part of opposing counsel. Here are a few of the most common problems we see in video depositions:

1. The witness is placed in front of a window, so she ends up looking dark and gloomy.

2. The witness is seated in front of a plant. The plant is distracting and even comical.

3. The witness is placed in front of a busy hallway, so you see people walking by and staring into the camera. As incredible as this sounds, we've seen several depositions in which this happened. Usually, they involved a doctor or other professional at his or her office, and there was a window facing a hallway, behind the person's desk.

4. The witness is seated *facing* a busy hallway, so she keeps looking at the people walking by. On the tape she looks distracted, shifty, and not credible.

5. The witness is lit by one single light source from above, darkening her eyes and making her look tired or even sinister.

6. The videographer zooms in or out during the testimony, adding unintentional emphasis and meaning to the testimony.

7. The camera is placed too low or too high, making the witness look either big and burly or small and insignificant.

You must ensure that your witness is not caught on tape for all time looking sinister, unconfident, or dishonest. Take control of the room, ensuring that she is not being made to look less than credible. Some of the finest trial lawyers we've worked with have walked out on depositions rather than allow their witnesses to look bad on tape.

A good professional videographer will bring a neutral backdrop, additional lighting, and a good exterior microphone. He or she will have no problem letting you look at your witness through the camera to make sure she looks good. But many times, you'll show up for the deposition and find an amateur with a video camera. In those cases, stand your ground, and do what you must to ensure a good tape. Here are a few hints:

Seating arrangements

- Position your witness so that she is neither directly in front of nor looking at a busy hallway with people walking by. If she starts watching the people, even when she is not speaking, she will become distracted and may answer a question that she did not hear properly. She may also look distracted and dishonest on the tape; remember that the audience viewing the tape won't know what she was looking at.

- In a typical conference room, with windows into the hallway on one side and outside windows on the other, we'll try to put the witness at one end of the table, and the examiner and camera on the side of the table toward the outside windows. That way, the light from the outside windows adds light to the witness's face, since she is facing that way to listen to the question and address the camera or the examiner (see "Preparing witnesses for deposition," page 165 below). Also, if anyone is distracted by the inside hallway, it will be opposing counsel rather than your witness.

■ If there is anything behind your witness (a painting, flowers, office equipment, telephone, or the like), ask to have it removed for the deposition.

Framing the witness

■ The camera should be positioned behind the examiner, as close to an over-the-shoulder shot as you can get without getting the examiner in the picture. This way, if the witness is looking at the examiner (see below), he will be looking in an area close to the camera lens. A head-on shot is the most persuasive. However, since you can not control the movements of the examiner— he or she may lean forward, sit back, and so on—you are limited in how head-on you are able to place the camera. In any case, try to position the camera to make it as easy as you can for the witness to look at or near the camera lens. Don't let the camera be positioned to the side of the witness. It makes it very difficult for the witness to look into the camera lens, and it makes it hard for the viewers to gauge the witness' credibility, because they can only see half of her face.

■ The camera should be placed slightly above the witness's eye level. If it is placed too low, the witness will look big, burly, generally unattractive, and possibly intimidating. If it is placed too high, the witness will look small, insignificant, unconfident, and possibly uncertain.

- The frame should be filled with the witness's head, shoulders, and arms (approximately table-level to just above her head).

- Once you have all agreed on the frame, make sure the videographer locks that position and will not zoom in or out. If he needs to adjust the frame, he should interrupt the testimony, not adjust it while the witness is speaking *or listening to the examiner.* Any camera movement sends a message to the viewer, and you do not want a purely unintentional camera move to affect how your witness's testimony is perceived by jurors.

Lighting

- Many conference rooms have only overhead lighting. This can cause shadows on the witness' face that can make her look tired, frustrated, or even sinister. To eliminate these shadows, you need what is known as a "fill light," a light source that fills in the shadows caused by the "key light," or main light source.

- In some rooms, outside windows can provide enough fill light to make the witness look good, provided that he is positioned facing the windows. Make sure that if the windows are on one side of his face, he does not have one side that is bright and one that is dark and shadowy.

- We have several clients who always go to depositions they're defending with a small gooseneck table lamp in the trunk of their car. That way, if they are faced with poor lighting, they can provide a quick and easy solution. Just aim the lamp at the witness to fill in any dark shadows.

Remember to look at your witness *through the camera lens* before the deposition begins. She may look great to you when you're sitting next to her, but look like she has a black eye when you look through the lens. Don't leave this responsibility to the videographer; take control of the way your witness is captured on tape. Don't be afraid to take control of the room and demand a better angle, better lighting, and a less distracting background. After all, once it's on tape, you're stuck with it.

Preparing witnesses for depositions

When preparing for deposition, every lawyer knows that preparation is key. Yet, our experience tells us that time and time again, lawyers put off the preparation till the very last minute, many times leaving only a couple of hours to prepare for one of the most important aspects of trial. Remember, it is much easier to prepare your witness for the deposition than it is to "fix" bad answers at trial. If you've prepared many witnesses for deposition over the course of your career, this information may not be new to you. However, we've tried to bring a non-lawyer's perspective to witness preparation and have found over the years that most witnesses need a more detailed lesson than even the most experienced lawyers give them.

A good witness preparation session teaches the witness how to deal with the entire deposition process. It leaves the witness capable of handling any question, not just the ones you "practiced." It involves listening skills, *never* memorized answers. If the witness is thinking, "Wait, I know we covered this ... what was that answer again?", while a question is being asked, then the prep session was not effective. He or she should never be thinking about what the "right" answer is. The witness should only be thinking about the question that was asked and the most honest answer to it.

Many times, when we are called in to help with the preparation of a "problem witness," the problem comes from some kind of miscommunication between the attorney and the witness. The witness is usually trying to avoid being "tricked" by the examiner, "win" the case during the deposition, or beat the examiner at his or her own game. A good witness preparation session cures more than just the symptoms of the witness's behavior; it also finds the underlying cause of the problem.

Before you begin to prepare your witness, you must first define your goals for the deposition. Are you hoping to encourage the other side to settle, or are you hoping to provide them with as little information as possible? Will the deposition be video taped or merely "on paper"? If the other side is deposing your expert, how much of your preparation is discoverable and, therefore, how much information do you want to disclose or keep from that expert? How does this witness's story fit in to the picture as a whole? Where does what he or she knows really count, and where does it not?

When you begin preparing the witness, remember that we learn and retain new information more effectively in an interactive session than in a lecture. If you begin with a long "lesson" about the do's and don'ts of depositions, you may have to repeat yourself quite a bit during the preparation session. Conversely, your witness retains more of the lesson if you ask questions and engage him or her in the lesson. For example, if the witness has testified before, you might ask, "What was the experience like for you? Were there any things that surprised you? Was there anything that happened that you want to avoid this time around?" If the witness has never testified, you might ask, "Is there anything about this deposition that makes you feel apprehensive?" A good question for any witness is "What information are you hoping the examiner won't ask you about? Is there anything that you did or didn't do that makes you feel embarrassed, or that you don't want to talk about?"

Good preparation is basically comprised of three essential elements for the witness:

- A thorough understanding of the case theory and overall themes;

- The ability to communicate the case theory and overall themes;

- Skills to avoid common traps and pitfalls.

Understanding the case theory and overall themes

Your witness must understand the theory of the case and its themes—in other words, what's the story, what really happened, why are we here? Many times, your client or your key witnesses have no clear understanding as to what you are attempting to communicate at deposition. Your client has an emotional reason for being there, but that emotion must be harnessed and released at just the right moments. In addition, they rarely know what needs to be communicated from a legal standpoint, for that is usually none of their concern.

By taking time to communicate the case theory and themes, you achieve two important goals:

1. You develop the "buy-in" from witnesses that will be necessary at trial, which is especially important when preparing expert witnesses.

2. You provide your witnesses with a safety net. Once you have discussed your themes and theories, ask witnesses to restate in their own words what they think your key themes are. Let them know that those themes (in their words, not yours) are points that they can loop back to throughout the deposition, whenever it seems appropriate.

The ability to communicate the theory and themes

This part is where we are most often called in to help out an attorney, for this is where the communication style of your witness is quite important. By now, you have thoroughly discussed the theory and the theme. What language will you use to express it? Ultimately, you want your witness to use his or her own language, not the exact words that you would use, or something he or she has tried to memorize. If the deposition will be videotaped, review the "Preparing witnesses for video depositions" section below. If the deposition is not being videotaped, focus on *listening skills* rather than "presentation skills." (See Chapter 10.)

Teach your witness how to listen to the question, and realize that he will improve with practice. Practice using direct and cross-examination questions, until you have achieved a level of consistency. Don't forget to teach your witness *how* to do what you're asking him to do. Many witnesses are told to answer only the question they are asked, but few are taught how to do it. This is a difficult concept for many witnesses to master. They are told to "be open and honest," to "tell their story," but then they are told to "keep their answers short." They are told to "listen to the question and correct any misconceptions in the question," but then they are told "not to argue with the examiner."

To make this concept easier for the witness to comprehend, tell them that you want them to tell the truth, the whole truth, and nothing but the truth. Telling the whole truth may mean correcting part of the question, or expanding on an answer, but if a further explanation is being offered only as an excuse for the answer, then it will sound defensive. In that case, the examiner will just ask the question again and again, and the witness will usually dig himself into a deeper and deeper hole. Explain the difference between giving a complete answer and making an excuse for an answer.

Q1. Then you offered Mr. Green the "other job" as you call it, in a completely different department, right?

A1. Yes.

Q2. And this was the same job that four other executives had already been shuffled into on their way out the front door, right?

A2. Four people had been offered the job but had not taken the position.

Q3. And you knew that Mr. Green wouldn't take the job either, because it was an empty position, just a stopping place for people on their way out of the company. You never really expected him to take the job, did you?

A3. The job was an excellent one, with equal pay and title to what Mr. Green had been receiving before, and offered a better opportunity for him to advance within the company. So, yes, I thought he would want the job.

Notice that question 1 only requires a "yes or no" response. If the witness had tried to "excuse" his answer by saying, "it was a good job," the examiner would simply get to reiterate her point: "It was in a completely different department than the one Mr. Green was hired for, right? It had completely different duties than the ones Mr. Green was trained to do and hired to do, right?" When the answer is simply "yes," train your witness to say it with confidence and clarity. With no trace of embarrassment, contrition, or uncertainty.

Question 2 held an incorrect implication, which the witness corrected calmly and politely. Question 3 was similar, but also required a "yes or no" answer. Without that final "yes," the examiner would simply rephrase and ask the question again. Without the explanation prior to the "yes," the examiner would also get the opportunity to rephrase her question and ask it differently: "yes, you expected him to take a job that was outside his training and expertise, and that no one else wanted?" Note that the explanation comes first, not the "yes." There are few things worse than the "yes, but…" answer. Even if the examiner doesn't cut the witness off before the explanation is complete, the witness will certainly sound defensive and unconvincing.

Skills to avoid common traps and pitfalls

Most witnesses feel apprehensive about the deposition process. They worry that they will say something wrong or that "loses the case." They worry that the examiner will try to "trap" them or twist their words. The best way to reassure them is through practice. Make sure they know what to expect and that they have experienced—and found a way out of—the particular situation they fear the most.

For some witnesses, it begins with the way they sit. Actors know that if you sit in a way that looks confident, your confidence grows. If you sit in a way that looks defensive or evasive, you will feel defensive or evasive and your answers will reflect that feeling. If you have a witness who slouches back in his chair, seems defensive or abrasive, or has an "attitude problem," sometimes all it takes to fix the attitude is to change the way he or she is sitting. Tell the witness to sit forward with a straight back, and clasped hands resting on the table. This is a strong, available, and confident position. That confidence will come through in the witness's testimony. Remind the witness to maintain this position no matter what the examiner does; this will help to eliminate the nonverbal cues or "tells" that signal when the examiner has "scored a hit" or otherwise made the witness feel uncomfortable.

Many witnesses go into a deposition thinking that they can "win" the deposition or that they can outsmart or outmaneuver the examiner. They see it as a battle, but they don't know what their ammunition really is. Remember the classic scene from *Raiders of the Lost Ark*, where the villain's henchman swings his sword around in an elaborate show of skill, only to have Indiana Jones look at him, unholster his pistol, and take him down in a single shot. Don't let your witnesses go into battle swinging madly with a sword only to get swiftly shot down. Arm them with the skills they'll need to come through unscathed.

1. **Tell the truth.** Everyone knows how important it is to tell the witness to tell the truth. But then the witness is told "Don't volunteer information, don't say that, don't imply this, don't, don't, don't … ." What does "tell the truth" mean? It means that you don't hedge, you don't fudge, you don't try to make the truth "sound better." It means that you don't try to justify, explain, or clarify the answer. You just answer, honestly and *briefly.*

2. **It's not your job to "win" the case with this deposition.** Many witnesses want to "win" the case in their deposition. They want to protect their company or themselves. No matter what they say to the contrary, most lay witnesses are either scared to death that they

will screw up and lose the case in their deposition or secretly hope that opposing counsel walks out of the deposition and says, "Oh, boy. We'd better settle this thing because we just don't have a chance!" Make sure you explain the process, your goals, and the realities of what can and cannot happen after the deposition. Make sure that witnesses know that they are not supposed to try to win the case in deposition and that their job is to listen to and answer honestly the questions they are asked.

3. **Answer only the question you are asked.** It seems simple enough, but this skill requires practice. It is not, after all, the way we interact in "real life." In real life, if someone asks you, "Do you know what time it is?", you typically say something like, "Oh, yes, it's 4:30." In a deposition, the response to that question should be "Yes." Explain the difference to the witness. Explain that it is not his or her responsibility to educate the examiner; if he or she wants to know what time it is, he or she will have to ask that question. During your prep session, look for situations in which the witness answers a question different from the one being asked. One common mistake goes something like this:

> **Q:** What did you do when you hung up the phone after that conversation?
>
> **A:** I thought maybe Mr. Smith had misunderstood me.

The question what not "What did you *think?*"; rather, it was "What did you *do?*" They are two very different questions. Train your witness to listen for the active verb, and answer *that* question. In this example, the witness might have answered something like "I called my wife," or I went to lunch," to indicate what he *did*.

4. **Don't discuss things that are outside your immediate experience.** The witness needs to know that it is okay to say, "I don't know."

5. **Read every document before you answer questions about it.** Many witnesses will not want to take the time to read a document, especially when they think they know what it is and what it says. Remind them that they should never feel rushed, that it is not their problem if the examiner runs out of time, and that it is important to be sure they are answering questions about the correct document—and the correct version of it.

6. **Take your time.** In preparing for depositions, witnesses should get into the habit of taking a second or two before answering every question. During this moment, they should make sure that they understand the question. Doing so gives you, the attorney, the opportunity to object, and it helps witnesses avoid falling into a dangerous rhythm. Make witnesses aware of the rhythm that can be created with closed-ended questions. Train them to notice when a rhythm of "yes" or "no" answers has begun, and how to stop it. Tell them

to pause, take a breath, think about what the examiner has asked, and then answer appropriately.

You must prepare witnesses for the *silences* involved in questioning, just as you would prepare them for the questions. Practice this exercise:

- **Ask and listen.** During preparation, ask your witness a question, and wait while she responds.

- **Do not take responsibility for the silence.** When she has finished her answer, do not take responsibility for filling the silence. If the witness answers your question and you do not jump right into the next question, but you look down at your notes or otherwise break contact with her, *you are taking the responsibility for the conversation onto yourself.* If you continue to look at her, and continue to place the burden of the conversation upon *her,* she will feel the need to fill the silence you have created. This can be as simple as maintaining eye contact with her and looking to her for the "rest" of the answer.

- **Try and try again.** If she falls into your trap and embellishes, stop her, explain what you are trying to teach her, and keep throwing this exercise into your questioning until she can recognize it when it happens. She must be able to refuse responsibility for filling the silences.

7. **Don't try to second-guess the examiner.** Remind the witness that this is what opposing counsel does for a living, and that the system is set up to help him get the information he needs to put together his case. The witness will never beat him at his own game. Being cooperative will always gain the witness more ground than will trying to "win." Train the witness to stop trying to figure out "where he is going with that question"—and to just answer the question. Remind her: if she doesn't answer the question, the examiner will just keep asking it until she does.

8. **Listen, listen, listen.** Explain to the witness that this is her job during the deposition. Most bad answers happen because the witness wasn't truly listening. They either misunderstood the question, didn't listen to an objection, or started trying to figure out where the examiner was going with the questions and answered a question that had not been asked yet.

Preparing witnesses for video depositions

If the depositions are being videotaped, your witnesses need presentation skills in addition to the skills discussed above. We recommend using a video camera during prep. This allows witnesses to get used to having a camera in the room focused on them and gives you the opportunity to see what they look like through the lens. However, it's usually best NOT to put any tape in the camera; because there may be discoverability issues, particularly with an expert witness, having a tape could be risky.

If you need to use a tape as a teaching tool for your witness, consider erasing the tape afterwards.

Moreover, unless you have an extraordinary amount of time to work with your witnesses, showing them video tapes of themselves will only serve to make them more self-conscious than they already are. It takes people awhile to get used to watching themselves on video tape, and to view their performances objectively and constructively. We recommend instead that you ask your witnesses to trust you when you tell them that something looks good or bad. It means that you have to work a bit harder to find a way to explain what behaviors you find ineffective, rather than just playing the video tape and saying "See what you're doing here?" But this extra work is preferable to having a self-conscious witness.

Presentation skills for video deposition

To prepare witnesses for video depositions, we start by teaching them how to sit. They are going to need to sit calmly and confidently, and make sure they are not doing anything that distracts from their message. They will need to be able to maintain that position for an extended period of time. To accomplish this, we tell witnesses to sit forward, with their arms resting on the table, and their hands clasped together. Research confirms that jurors rate witnesses who sit in this position as more credible than witnesses who sit back in their chairs, even if they are sitting up straight. Sitting with hands clasped also helps to avoid making distracting gestures. On camera, with a tight frame, even small gestures look enormous.

Unfortunately, this forward and upright position can put strain on a person's back and make one tend to slouch or fidget. To make it easier to maintain this posture, tell witnesses to sit *far* forward on the front of their chairs. This will help to take the strain off the lower back, and enable them to maintain this position for a longer period of time. (For a demonstration on witness posture, see the enclosed CD-ROM).

> **NOTE:** It is not enough to tell your witnesses what *not* to do. You must also tell them what *to* do. Give them active skills to solve the problems you observe through the camera lens. For example, if a witness tends to swivel in her chair or fidget with her feet, have her anchor both feet flat on the floor, or bring her feet further under the chair. Find what works to help her lock her legs in place, and make the position more comfortable.

The most common question we get about preparing a witness for video depositions is, "should the witness look at the camera?" Our answer is, "it depends on the witness."

Making eye contact through a camera lens is extremely difficult for most people. Sometimes, you look into the lens and see a black hole. Sometimes, with a professional camera, you look into the lens and see yourself upside down, which can be very disconcerting. That said, witnesses—especially experts who are trying to "teach" the jury via video—are significantly more credible and effective if they can master this skill. When a witness can successfully speak directly to the camera, the viewer becomes a more active participant in the process.

For this reason, we recommend that you try to teach your witness how to make eye contact with the camera, just as you would teach him how to make eye contact with the jury during his testimony at trial. For example, tell your witness to turn his chair to face the camera, so he has to turn his head to look at the examiner, but looking at the camera requires no extraneous movement. The very position of his chair will make it *easier* for him to look at the camera than at the examiner.

Sometimes a witness is able to learn the physical skill of looking at the lens, but appears like the proverbial deer in the headlights when he does so. He isn't able to *communicate* with the camera lens as he can communicate with a live person. In that case, you may want to ask him to use a different technique. You may want to ask him to share the information between the questioner and the lens. In other words, ask him to talk to the questioner *and* to the lens, as if it were another person in the room. He needs to practice until he is talking more conversationally with the camera, and including the camera as much as he includes the questioner.

If the witness still does not look comfortable including the camera, or if you do not have time for him to practice the skill of talking to the camera, then you'll have to advise him to look at the examiner. In that case, placement of the camera becomes even more important. If the camera is placed to the side of the witness, then the viewer can only see half of the witness's face during his testimony. (See "Framing the witness," above).

Preparing witnesses for trial

If you prepared any of your witnesses for "paper" depositions (as opposed to a video depositions), then the first thing you'll want to tell them when you begin preparing for trial is to forget what you told them to do in the deposition. Many attorneys seem stumped as to why their witnesses are so closed-off and "difficult" when they begin prepping for trial. "It's like pulling teeth to get her to tell her story!" they have complained to us. Often, that is because the witness remembers the attorney clearly saying "keep your answers as brief as possible, never volunteer any information, and pause before you answer each question." It seems obvious, but many attorneys forget to tell the witness that this process—the process of trial—is different from the deposition process.

Begin by teaching your witness how to sit—forward on the chair, if possible with her hands clasped on the rail in front of her. Tell her what the chair will be like in the box, what the microphone will be like. Teach her to walk to the chair, sit down, turn the chair to face the jury (or to split the difference between the lectern and the bench, in the case of a bench trial), turn the microphone so it is pointed toward her mouth, and "assume the position." It is very important that she remember to turn her chair to face the jury, because it will make it much more likely that she will talk to the jurors, instead of to you or opposing counsel. It should be easier for her to look at the jurors than at the questioner. She should need to turn her head to look at the questioner, but look straight ahead of her to connect with the jurors.

Eye contact in a jury trial

It is extremely important that your witnesses learn to connect with the jurors as they answer every question—on direct examination and on cross-examination. Some attorneys ask us, "Doesn't it look unnatural and contrived if a witness looks at the jurors every time he answers a question?" No—surprisingly, it doesn't. Jury researchers confirm that witnesses who look at the jury when answering are consistently rated as more credible than those who do not (Dr. Karen Lisko, Ph.D., doctoral thesis). The jurors very quickly accept the convention. Teach your witness to look at the questioner and listen very carefully to the question, then look at the jurors when answering.

It is important for witnesses to look at the jurors every time they answer. Even if the answer is just, "Yes." Obviously, it is easier to look at the jurors during longer answers than during shorter ones. Suggest to your witness that it will feel more comfortable answering "Yes, I did," or "Yes, that's correct," instead of just the one-word "Yes." There are a couple of benefits to doing this. First, it feels more comfortable. Second, it diminishes the tendency to fall into a "yes" rhythm on cross-examination.

To make looking at the jurors more comfortable for your witnesses, explain the following:

> Remember, I already know the answers to the questions I'm asking you on direct examination. Mr. Jones already knows the answers to the questions he's asking you on cross-examination. The

only people who don't know the answers are the jurors. It's all about them. So tell them what you need them to know.

When we explain this to witnesses, they usually pick up the skill very quickly. So while you are preparing your witnesses, we suggest having at least two people in the room who can act as "jurors" to give the witnesses a setting in which to practice this skill.

You should also reiterate the importance of maintaining their demeanor as you prepare your witnesses for cross-examination. Think about your goals for this particular witness. If she is a corporate defendant, you may want her to look at the jury for every answer on cross to build rapport and credibility. If she is a plaintiff fighting the evil corporate lawyer, you may want her to look at opposing counsel on cross to make the jurors feel the need to "rescue" her from the attacking lawyer.

Once you have determined your goals, teach your witness in a way that takes into account her natural desire to "win." For instance:

> Don't fall into the trap of looking at Mr. Jones (opposing counsel) on cross. That is what Mr. Jones wants. He wants you to change your demeanor. To become wary, cautious, finicky, even hostile. And he wants you to interact with *him,* not with the jurors. If he can achieve that change in your demeanor, he has succeeded in damaging your credibility. Don't let that happen. Don't let him get what he wants.

For witnesses who have a tendency to fall into a verbal "battle of wits" on cross, who clearly want to "win" this exchange, explain that the way to win on cross-examination is by maintaining their demeanor. Remind them again—they are talking to the *jurors,* not the cross-examiner, and they should feel no hostility toward *them.*

Eye contact in a bench trial

In the case of a bench trial, you probably don't want your witnesses looking at the judge for every answer. For one thing, the judge will take notes, or look over an exhibit, or otherwise be unavailable to make eye contact. It may be very disconcerting for witnesses if they keep trying to look at the judge and the judge isn't making eye contact in return.

In preparing for bench trials, we teach witnesses to *share the information with the judge,* answering both the questioner and the judge, and talking to both equally. In some courtrooms, the bench is so far back that it seems to be behind the witness stand. In that case, the witnesses will need to turn the witness chair to split the difference between the questioner and the bench. They should then look at the questioner during each question, listen very carefully to the question being asked, then include both the judge and the questioner in their answers. It is important to practice this skill.

Witness Preparation
Worksheet

[**Note:** An electronic copy of this worksheet is included on the CD-ROM in the "Worksheets" folder.]

For Deposition:

1. Will the deposition be on video? _____

   Why: _____

2. What are your goals for this deposition?

   _____

   _____

3. What is your witness going to wear for the video deposition? Remember: avoid the color red, small or flashy prints, jewelry, watches, and so forth.

   _____

   _____

4. List the themes your witness can loop back to (using his or her own words):

   _____

   _____

5. Is your witness going to make eye contact with the camera, the examiner, or both?

   _____

   _____

6. Notes and observations:

_____

_____

For Trial:

1. What are your goals for this testimony?

_____

_____

2. What is your witness going to wear to court?

_____

_____

3. List the themes your witness can loop back to (using his or her own words):

_____

_____

4. What elements of the environment should the witness be made aware of (i.e., swivel chair, microphone, distance to the jury box, and so forth)?

_____

_____

5. Notes and observations:

_____

_____

The Deposition You're Taking
Worksheet

[**Note:** An electronic copy of this worksheet is included on the CD-ROM in the "Worksheets" folder.]

1. Will the deposition be on video? _____

   Why: _____

2. What are your goals for this deposition?

   _____

   _____

3. For a discovery deposition, outline your story, identifying each "chapter" or "vignette." Leave blank bullet points to represent the details you don't know, that will fill out the story.

   _____

   _____

4. What questions will you ask to find out the information you're missing to create a compelling and credible story?

   _____

   _____

5. When and how will you ask these questions (sometimes a linear line of questioning is not the most effective way to get information.)

   _____

   _____

6. What information do you need to walk out the door with, in order to support your motions?

_____

_____

7. Notes and observations:

_____

_____

Chapter 13:
Trial Day 1: What To Wear?

What you wear in court obviously influences the way the jurors perceive you. Clearly, you want them to perceive you as professional, and reasonably successful.

What constitutes "professional" attire varies widely by region. A pair of polished cowboy boots is quite acceptable in Ft. Worth, but frowned upon in Dallas, just 45 minutes away. In some courtrooms in the South, women are expressly forbidden by the judge to wear pants, no matter how tailored and professional they may be.

Know your venue

Know your neighbors. Know your jury pool and what they view as professional. A few years ago in Silicon Valley, where the technological "gold rush" was making millionaires faster than you could say "Internet startup," your double-breasted Armani suit might have been just the ticket in the courtroom. But if the economy is stagnant, it is vitally important to avoid looking "slick." Don't overdress in such a way that it suggests that you're just in it for the money. Don't confirm the negative stereotype or bad lawyer jokes by the way you dress. You want to go for professional, classic, and successful, not "rich," "slick," or "greedy."

Feeling comfortable

Obviously, you want to feel comfortable in what you're wearing. An outfit that is in opposition with your personal style is going to make you feel self-conscious, doing more harm than good. But what makes you most comfortable may not be appropriate for the venue. Many of us require an outside opinion. Ask someone you trust—a spouse, a colleague, or a paralegal in your office—if you question whether your outfit is appropriate for court.

Bejeweled and bedecked

Avoid wearing any accessory that is distracting. If jurors are busy admiring (or coveting) that rock on your finger, they're not listening to what you have to say. Leave your wedding ring on. Men should avoid all other jewelry and choose a conservatively patterned necktie. Likewise, women should be very conservative in their choice of earrings, pins, scarves, and other accessories.

A few guidelines

■ Don't wear *anything* that costs more than most of your jurors will make in a month. Wear a neat, professional suit (or even sport jacket and slacks, depending upon your venue).

■ Know your venue: what the community perceives as professional, what the median income level is, and so forth. Dress appropriately.

- Don't wear anything that is diametrically opposed to your normal style. If you're a woman who usually wears low heels, don't wear three-inch pumps for the courtroom, no matter how stylish they look.

- Don't wear anything that attracts more attention than your argument. Ally McBeal notwithstanding, short skirts and fluorescent ties are a poor choice.

- Don't dramatically change your look mid-trial. If the jurors are faced with a completely new image to reconcile with your old one, your credibility will be questioned.

Chapter 14:
Using Props And Visual Aids In Order To Enhance Your Argument

Many lawyers ask us how we feel about using visual aids—charts, graphs, PowerPoint presentations, and other demonstrative exhibits—in the courtroom. The rule of thumb is this: use visual aids to enhance or advance your argument, not to replace your argument. Good visual aids can improve juror retention of information, clarify information, appeal to different jurors with different learning styles, and generally add excitement to the trial. Bad visual aids can cause confusion and frustration, and undermine your credibility.

So often we see attorneys spend lots of money on the "perfect" visual aid, or the newest high-tech video image, feeling that the jury needs to be entertained with "eye candy" at all times. However, their time and their client's money are usually better spent if they give more thought to the oral presentation of the facts. Putting in the time to develop a persuasive and compelling oral argument will often lead you to more powerful visual aids. Money is not always the key to a great demonstrative exhibit. If having the flashiest visual aids were the key to determining who wins and who looses in the courtroom, then it would follow that those with the most expensive visual aids always win. We all know that isn't the case.

In many cases, the jurors will benefit from a broad range of media—from a flip chart, to a video, to a PowerPoint presentation—to illustrate different points. Use the medium that is most appropriate for what you are trying to accomplish with a particular exhibit. Don't forget to learn how to use the media you employ. If the technology doesn't work or you get thrown off of your argument because you don't feel comfortable using the medium, then you may do yourself more harm than good.

Demonstrative exhibits should do what their name implies: *demonstrate* what you are discussing. They should make it easier for the jurors to understand your argument: to "see" your picture (see Chapter 6). If you design your demonstratives with that in mind, you'll use them well.

One of the most common problems we see happens when the attorney designs the demonstrative to convey all the information that the attorney thinks is important, instead of designing it with the juror in mind. The exhibit ends up with so much information crammed into it that no one farther than a foot away can read any of it. This is not just annoying for the jurors: it can make them angry. We've heard more than one mock juror complain that:

> "The lawyer made the words so small that we couldn't read it. He must have been trying to hide something from us. If he had really wanted us to see the whole thing, he would have blown it up so we could see it. What was he hiding?"

Some of the best demonstrative exhibits we've seen have been used to illustrate patterns of behavior or to establish timelines. Obviously, you should enlarge important documents and highlight, or "call out," key information. But remember to let the jurors see the name of the document, and the document as a whole, before you show them the highlighted portions. They need to understand the function and significance of the document you are quoting from and see that you are not trying to hide the rest of the document or inappropriately use a quote out of context.

One effective demonstrative that is often overlooked is the jury instructions. It can be very effective to enlarge certain jury instructions that are key to your case so you can explain them to the jurors in closing arguments.

If you learn how to use them, PowerPoint and Trial Director can be great tools in the courtroom. However, don't forget about the creative use of low-tech exhibits. Writing information yourself as you explain it—on a blackboard or flip chart—can be extremely effective. We all went through school watching our teachers do just that, and we tend to give some credence to information that is written right in front of us. Also, it adds spontaneity—or at least the impression of it—to the courtroom.

Another advantage to some low-tech exhibits is that you can leave them up for the jurors to see. A timeline might be more effective on a large poster board, rather than on a PowerPoint slide, so that you can leave it up and refer to it consistently throughout your opening statement, rather than needing to flip back and forth to the slide.

When you sit down after writing something on a flip chart or using an important poster board exhibit, leave it right where it is. In a surprising number of cases, opposing counsel doesn't remove the exhibits. The exhibits stay right there, reminding the jury of your argument throughout opposing counsel's argument. Whatever you do, however, don't fall into this trap yourself. Always remove any opposing exhibits before you speak.

From a presentation perspective, it comes down to this: make sure the exhibit is created with the jurors—not you or your client—in mind. Ask yourself, "Does this exhibit enhance my argument, or am I trying to use it in place of my argument?"

Chapter 15:
Presentation Skills For Voir Dire

Ask yourself what you really want to achieve in voir dire. Is your goal to find out where the potential jurors live, what they do for a living, and how many kids they have, and to write all of that down on your legal pad? Or is your goal to find out about their *value system*, their core beliefs that may make them unable to treat your client fairly, or give her the money you think she deserves, or punish those who hurt her? Is your goal to teach them about the legal system? Or is it to establish yourself as someone they can trust, someone they can look to for answers when they don't understand what is happening in the courtroom?

To build a relationship with the jurors during voir dire, you must be willing to put aside your notes and have a human interaction. You must be willing to make honest eye contact. You must be able to express your vulnerability and your desire to know them as human beings, not just as potential jurors #1 – #25. This process involves more than knowing their names; it involves *listening*.

Many attorneys come into voir dire with the desire to make the jurors *like* them. We would like to amend that. We think your goals in voir dire should be much more specific:

1. Find out who is going to hurt you in the jury room.

2. *Listen* to the jurors.

3. Build relationships with the jurors.

There are two common communication mistakes we see attorneys making in voir dire: (1) being too ingratiating, and (2) not listening. Many times, these two mistakes are intertwined. Some lawyers are so afraid that the jurors won't like them that they don't ask any questions deeper than, for example, "Do you like being a dentist, Mr. Smith?" Then the lawyer smiles sweetly and makes a comment about how much they like their own dentist. This type of ingratiating behavior doesn't work, nor is it necessary. You do not need to be *liked* to win your case. You need to be respected and viewed as honest and credible. People are rarely impressed by someone trying to impress them. They are impressed by someone who truly listens to them, truly engages them in conversation, values their opinions, and is honestly interested in who they are as human beings. If they feel that you honestly care about what they have to say, you'll get more information and build a much deeper relationship.

Other attorneys are so afraid of voir dire that they rush through a list of questions, not really listening to the answers. They are terrified of having a conversation with potential jurors, so concerned they'll get a "bad answer" that they fail to get any useful information at all. They're so afraid of someone hurting their case during voir dire that they fail to discover who will hurt their case during deliberations.

Having a conversation with prospective jurors requires some faith on your part. There certainly will be jurors who say things that are in opposition to your case. Those are precisely the people you must try to identify and possibly have excused during voir dire. Of course, if one were to say something like,

"Yes, I've had a bad experience with a doctor. *Your client* operated on my mother and botched her surgery, too," that person would likely be excused for cause, but only after he had already hurt your case. Thus, a better approach is to ask prospective jurors whether they have had any experience with the parties involved in the case before you get into your open-ended, value-oriented questions.

Most answers given in voir dire—no matter how much an attorney may inwardly wince upon hearing them—are not really going to contaminate the jury. People have their own opinions coming into voir dire; and most prospective jurors are not going to disassociate themselves from their own strong opinions simply by hearing the strong differing opinions of a stranger sitting next to them. If you get a bad answer, thank the juror for being honest and silently congratulate yourself for finding this dangerous juror while you can still do something about it. But don't forget to find out who else feels the same way:

> "Mr. Jones, thank you so much for talking so honestly with me. You obviously have some very strong opinions on this subject. By a show of hands, how many feel the same way as Mr. Jones?"

If you believe it is necessary to counter the answer, never do it yourself. Ask if anyone has a different opinion and let them explain. But be careful, and make sure you absolutely must do it, because you are revealing to the other side the people who might be best for you in the jury room. So, for example, if you already know that the other side is going to strike Juror Number Four because of some answers she gave earlier, then you might allow her to defend your position against the opinion expressed by Mr. Jones. Notice that the question above did not ask "Who feels the same way as Mr. Jones." By asking *how many,* you are telling them that it is okay, reasonable, and understandable for them to agree with the statement made by Mr. Jones.

Having a conversation with prospective jurors requires a leap of faith for another reason: When we get nervous, we find it hard to trust that we'll know what to say next; consequently, we tend to cling to our notes as if they will protect us. To have a conversation and build relationships with your jurors, you cannot just roll through your pre-planned questions. If you aren't listening to their answers, they might as well just fill out a questionnaire and be done with it. The jurors must feel that their answers affect you. If they perceive that your reaction won't change no matter what they say, then they are not going to relate to you on a fundamental human level. A conversation requires a give and take of information, not note-taking. So have someone else in the courtroom—a paralegal, secretary, co-counsel, or consultant—to take notes for you.

How prospective jurors see you listening to the other jurors can have great impact on how they relate to you when their turn comes along. If they perceive that you will listen to them and strive to understand, they will want to communicate with you. If they know that you will respect their answers, even if you disagree with them, they will be much more willing to be honest with you. If, on the other hand, they watch you ignoring or correcting other jurors' answers that you don't like, they will edit their own answers accordingly. If they know that revealing their biases against plaintiffs who sue for "pain and suffering" will result in some form of correction from you, do you think they will be as open and honest with you about their values and beliefs as you need them to be? If they perceive that you are more interested in taking notes than in truly listening to their answers, how important do you think they'll perceive their answers to be? And if their answers are not important to you, why should they open up enough to give you anything more than the politically correct response? If you roll over an open honest answer like an automaton pushing through your list of questions without responding as a human being, do you think that juror, or any of the others who watch this exchange, will view you as someone they can relate to?

Active listening during voir dire will elicit more detailed, honest answers (see Chapter 10). How many times have you seen an attorney ask his next question just as the prospective juror was opening her mouth to add to her answer? If you wait and *listen* for just a few seconds after the juror has finished speaking, you not only convey respect for that person; you also create a momentary silence that must be filled. If you don't fill it, the juror will. Many times, you will get much more honest, revealing, and useful information from a juror's attempt to fill the silence than from his or her original answer.

We realize that your time in voir dire is limited, but you'll give and receive more information in less time if there is a natural exchange and true communication. In our focus group work, this has been one of the most surprising lessons that attorneys learn. After conducting ten minutes of voir dire with the focus of engaging the jurors in a conversation, they suddenly realize that it is possible to get to know these jurors and to let the jurors know them. Once again, it all comes down to listening.

Practice the following techniques to increase your effectiveness in voir dire:

1. **Put down your notes.** If you want to address jurors by name, ask their names. This is what would happen in conversation, isn't it? When you must look at your notes, or take a note, do so between questions. Stop questioning while you write. Do not take notes or look at your notes while the juror is speaking.

2. **Take the time to look.** Before you begin speaking, make eye contact with each juror and acknowledge that contact. Eye contact is the single most effective way to initiate that relationship. It tells jurors right from the beginning that what they have to say is important. (Review our discussion of eye contact and techniques to improve it in Chapter 5.)

3. **Pause for three seconds.** After each answer, make sure the juror is finished speaking and provide him or her with the opportunity to "fill the silence." Three seconds may feel long to you, but it will not look long to your listeners. It will look respectful.

4. **Listen to and acknowledge each answer.** Never move to another question without acknowledging the previous answer. You may intend to come back to that juror,

but not acknowledging answers gives the impression that you are not listening, disapproved of the answer, or just don't care about the answers that they give you.

5. **Ask simple questions.** Don't ask a long, complicated question, then ask the whole panel what they think about it. This process is hard enough—jurors shouldn't also have to try to figure out what you are asking them. Keep your questions short and clear.

6. **Never contradict, ignore, or discourage any answer.** Thank the juror for being so candid. You must encourage the other jurors to be as open and honest with you as possible, not simply to give you the answers you want to hear.

Voir Dire
Worksheet

[**Note:** An electronic copy of this worksheet is included on the CD-ROM in the "Worksheets" folder.]

1. What are your goals with this voir dire?

   _____

   _____

2. What are the *values* or *life experiences* that are warning signs that the juror might be harmful to you and your case?

   _____

   _____

3. What questions are you going to ask to reveal those *values* and *life experiences?*

   _____

   _____

4. Are you *Taking the Time to Look* in voir dire, establishing contact before asking your questions, and giving the other person time to expand on his or her answer?

5. Notes and observations:

   _____

   _____

Chapter 16:
Preparing Your Opening Statement:
99 Percent Of Spontaneity Is Preparation

Some attorneys believe that to be spontaneous, you must be unrehearsed. A professional actor must rehearse for weeks, then do eight shows a week, every week, for five years. And the seventh show of the forty-ninth week of the fourth year must be just as spontaneous as opening night. Interestingly, most actors find they can be *more spontaneous* if they have rehearsed extensively. To be truly spontaneous, they must have prepared so completely that they can diverge from the script without worrying about forgetting the rest of the play.

Lawyers are taught not to memorize their opening statements or closing arguments. They are told that if you've memorized it, you can't react spontaneously or add or cut material at the last minute. Having performed on stage for most of our adult lives, we know that this is completely untrue. You can be truly spontaneous if you are not thinking about what to say next. If you don't need to think about *what* you are going to say, you are free to concentrate on *how* you say it, and how it affects your listener. You are free to focus on your audience rather than yourself. That said, we understand that attorneys usually don't have the time necessary to memorize an entire opening statement, nor is it usually necessary. Instead, what we recommend to our clients is to memorize the first few minutes of their opening statement. This ensures a strong first impression, and allows the attorney to get past the initial nerves while looking confident and prepared.

In addition to memorizing a strong beginning, you might want to memorize other sections of your opening. Chapters, or vignettes (see Chapter 7), that are exceptionally important, complex, or worrisome are easier to control if they are memorized. The more chapters you have down cold, the less anxiety you feel and the more free you are to react to arguments made by your opposition.

How to memorize text

Never try to memorize text by reading it to yourself. Actors memorize long speeches quickly and thoroughly. We do it not by *thinking* about the text but by speaking it aloud, over and over again, until we know it so well that we can say it quickly without forgetting what comes next. Just as you can learn to play a sport by repeating a movement over and over again until the movement becomes unconscious rather than conscious, you can learn text by speaking it until your subconscious can take over. When you reach that point, you know that even if you are distracted, nervous, or confused, the words will come out as you have rehearsed them.

An added bonus to this method is that when you hear yourself speaking, you will hear ways to make your delivery better. You will hear ways to change your vocal inflection (see Chapter 2), you will think of gestures to enhance your argument (see Chapter 4), you will think of new sensory words or details to add (see Chapter 7). You will hear what works and what doesn't.

The other secret to memorizing long text is having a thorough understanding of the context and meaning. In order to memorize a script, an actor must understand exactly why he is saying what he is saying, and how each thought connects to the next. In Hamlet's advice to the players, Shakespeare advises that an actor "connect the word to the action, the action to the word."

How to prepare your opening statement

1. **Outline your opening statement.** Remember the structure and elements covered in Part 2.

2. **Speak your opening statement** into a tape recorder, using your notes and outline. Feel free to say things like "Oh, that didn't work, strike that whole paragraph," or "Move this to the end." NOTE: It is important that you *speak* the statement before you write it. The way we write is not the same as the way we speak, and to make your statement more persuasive and easier to memorize, it should be written *to be spoken.* It is significantly harder to wrap your mouth around words that are written the way you *write* as opposed to the way you *speak.* By speaking aloud, you'll find key phrases—things you said just brilliantly on the tape—that you can then use in the final draft. Remember—this is *oral* argument.

3. **Have your assistant transcribe the tape.** Voice recognition software, such as Dragon® *Naturally Speaking* or IBM's *Via Voice,* provide a good alternative. They are rather accurate and can eliminate the need for a transcriber.

4. **Edit your statement on paper,** employing the "Six Elements of a Great Story" and the other storytelling skills discussed in Part 2 of this book.

5. **Memorize your introduction** and the first two or three minutes of your opening statement, using the technique discussed above.

6. **Memorize any other chapters,** vignettes, sections, sentences, or language that you want to make sure to get right.

7. **Create a "speaking outline."** Write an outline that lists the sections in order and contains a few key words for each section to jog your memory if you need it. Avoid complete sentences—you just want to jog your memory. Compose the outline in a 14-point or 16-point font so you can read it easily. Keep this outline on the lectern or counsel table, where you can use it during your opening statement. Look at it after each major section of your opening to make sure you don't forget something important and remind yourself which section comes next.

By memorizing this way, you give yourself plenty of opportunity to add new material, change the order of certain sections, or cut an entire section.

The key is, your opening statement can't be "sort of" memorized; it must be so well-memorized that you *never* have to think about what you are going to say next. That's the whole point. To do this, you *must* memorize it by speaking it aloud.

Just as your subconscious remembers to engage the clutch while you're driving, even when your brain is thinking about the fight you just had with your kids, your subconscious also remembers words you have spoken many times, even when your conscious brain can't.

So now that you have thoroughly prepared your opening, you are free to be spontaneous. If you are not struggling to compose your opening statement in the moment, you are free to listen. Being spontaneous is simply taking the time to listen and react to what happens in your environment. This spontaneity allows your opening statement to have the feeling of being told for the first time. This confidence and preparation allows you to connect with the jurors, which, in turn, makes them feel comfortable with you. Feeling comfortable is contagious. You learn that the best cure for stage fright is to prepare thoroughly and connect with your listeners.

Chapter 17:
Stage Fright

"I find speaking here [in Congress] and elsewhere about the same thing. I was about as badly scared, and no worse, as I am when I speak in court."

— Abraham Lincoln

The key to avoiding debilitating stage fright is preparation. Your confidence increases in relation to your level of preparedness. If you know that you can tell your story, you know the facts of the case, you know you have done all your homework, and you know that you have trained and warmed up your body and voice in a way that will enhance your performance, you dramatically reduce your stage fright. If you have memorized the key moments of your opening statement (see Chapter 16), you will feel more prepared than ever before.

Nonetheless, nerves creep in. That is just something that we humans, no matter how well-trained and experienced, will always have to deal with. We can, however, minimize the effect of our stage fright and turn it into a positive factor in our presentation.

Nerves are your ally

Fear can be thought of as energy, energy that can be converted into power. It brings excitement to the room.

Before you stand up to speak, when you feel those butterflies attacking your stomach, take a moment to acknowledge them. Try changing your perspective of them. Think to yourself "Oh, good, I'm *excited,*" instead of "Oh, no, I'm nervous." What do you think people are referring to when they talk about the "magic" of opening night? The *excitement* caused by the nerves of the performers adds electricity to the air. It's not magic; it's fear converted into excitement. If you take the time to acknowledge your fear and then begin to speak in spite of it, the fear recedes, and in its place, you feel power. Courage is not the absence of fear, but the ability to face your fear and, with knees shaking, go in there and do it anyway. It is inspiring to watch, and the personal rewards are countless.

Preparation, preparation, preparation

In terms of overcoming stage fright, there is really only one way to do that: preparation. Stage fright comes even after years of experience; no matter how many times we speak in front of groups, we still get nervous when we feel we didn't prepare as thoroughly as we know we should have. The key to preparation is practicing aloud. We're always brilliant and eloquent in our heads, but the first time we say something aloud, the change throws us off.

We've had a few clients with such terrifying stage fright that we have recommended that they memorize their entire opening. Memorization takes quite a bit of time and commitment, but it makes a *huge* difference in terms of stage fright. An excellent alternative is to memorize the first three or four minutes (see Chapter 16). These first few minutes are critical to the jurors' perceptions of you and your own comfort level. Once you feel comfortable, you can more easily switch to working from an outline. But if you feel totally prepared for those first few minutes, your stage fright is dramatically reduced. Even though we now feel very comfortable speaking to groups, we never get up to speak without having memorized the first few minutes of our presentation.

It is also essential that you warm up and get your blood flowing before you walk into the courtroom. After all, you would never consider running a race without warming up your body; why would you consider going into another physical activity, with significantly more at stake, without warming up your primary tool of persuasion: yourself?

The best way to overcome the stage fright that creeps in during your presentation is to change your focus: to your audience. Don't focus on whether they like you; focus on whether they understand the information you're offering. Focus on whether they hear what you're saying. Taking the focus off yourself will help you to work through those nerves that creep in when you get self-conscious.

Most importantly, remember that jurors are not necessarily a hostile audience. They are hoping to see something done well, something that warrants their trust, and they are not averse to liking you if given sufficient cause. They are very forgiving about the little things that make the speaker nervous, such as losing your place, losing your train of thought, and so on. In hundreds of post-trial juror interviews, we've never heard a juror say anything negative about an attorney because he or she momentarily got lost or tongue-tied. Even if we mention the moment in question (because the attorney was feeling terrible about it), the jurors rarely even remember it.

Don't try to cover up a mistake—use it

Many of the greatest trial lawyers we've worked with admit that they still get nervous before every trial. Nearly all of them have stories about great courtroom "disasters." What makes these lawyers great is that they know how to handle the fear—and the disasters—with grace.

One of the finest trial lawyers we know told us that at the beginning of one of his first trials, he stepped up to the lectern, and promptly spilled an entire pitcher of water all over himself, the lectern, his notes, and part of the floor:

> "I was petrified. I was sure the jurors would think I was inept, clumsy, or even just plain dumb. As I cleaned up the mess, I apologized to the jurors, told them how nervous I was that I wouldn't do a good job for my client, and asked them to please overlook my personal flaws as they look at the evidence in the case. After the jurors delivered a verdict in my favor, I thanked them, and apologized again for the bad first impression I had made. The jurors told me that I didn't need to apologize, that they had actually formed a very good impression of me, because I had admitted my fear and my anxiety. My admission had made them feel more connected to me, and made them pull for me throughout the trial."

Another client of ours claimed to have debilitating stage fright. He admitted to referring work—and even encouraging settlements—because he was afraid of going to trial. Finally, he realized that he couldn't avoid going to trial on a particular case and that he was going to have to give an opening statement. He worked very hard to prepare his presentation. He did all of the preparation we discuss in Chapter 16, even memorizing the first few minutes of his opening statement. He warmed up his voice and his body before he walked into the courtroom. All of this preparation made him feel capable of delivering his opening, but he still had those persistent butterflies. When he began his opening statement, he forgot to connect first to the jurors before speaking. He spoke a couple of sentences to the floor, then got tongue-tied. Suddenly, he stopped talking, looked up into the eyes of the jurors, took a deep breath, said "Excuse me," and began again. From that moment on, it was clear to everyone in the courtroom that this jury was pulling for this man—not out of pity, or even sympathy, but because he had shown his courage, vulnerability, and humanity.

The courtroom is one place you can be rewarded for admitting your fear.

What to do when you lose your place

If you truly know your story and you have rehearsed it so that you know the most important elements, you will never "lose your place." There may be times when you lose your train of thought and lose touch with the important point you were making. Things like this happen. It is normal, and it should not be a source of anxiety. After all, no one is impressed by the actor's ability to remember his or her lines. Use the silence to your advantage. A professional actor know that some of the most compelling and dramatic moments happen in the silence of the moment. Allow it, use it consciously as a tool, and don't fear it when it happens unexpectedly.

If you lose your place, follow these simple guidelines:

- If you lose your place, *stop.*

- Be silent as you regain your story. If you have followed our suggestions on memorization and preparation (Chapter 16), you can check your outline and regain your momentum within seconds.

- If you remain *present,* the audience will never know that you lost your place; they'll just be curious about what you'll say next.

- Don't let losing your place worry you. Remember, an occasional moment of awkward spontaneity is endearing.

Stage Fright
Worksheet

[**Note:** An electronic copy of this worksheet is included on the CD-ROM in the "Worksheets" folder.]

1. List the four steps to take when you "lose your place."

    _____

    _____

2. What changes can you make in the way you view public speaking, to help overcome your fear (i.e. realizing that jurors *want* to like you)?

    _____

    _____

3. How have you warmed up your body and voice, and otherwise prepared yourself for presentation to eliminate the fear that comes from a lack of preparation?

    _____

    _____

4. Notes and observations:

    _____

    _____

Chapter 18:
On-Camera Presentation Skills

The new millennium brings with it new tools and new challenges for the trial lawyer: the attorneys, the witnesses, even the judge may appear in the courtroom via television or videotape. From the Microsoft case to the presidential debates, it has become clear that *how you say it* on camera can—and will—be used against you. Many cases still come down to the effectiveness of the *argument*. How the jurors perceive the "virtual argument" is affected by entirely different criteria than a "live argument." Some litigators are mastering the new technology available to them, but it is not enough to learn how to use this new technology to present evidence to a jury. A poor deposition caught on video or a poor appearance via closed-circuit television can cause a good case to look bad.

The human contact factor: making the connection through a camera lens

Speaking to a camera lens is quite different from speaking live to a group of people.

We've discussed many times in *The Lawyer's Winning Edge* the importance of connecting to your audience, listener, or the trier of fact. When we connect to another individual, we have someone to react to. We "listen" to their verbal and non-verbal responses. It is an active exchange. In front of the camera, however, this critical human contact is missing.

It is important that as the speaker, you make the viewer feel that this human contact is *not* missing, that you are connecting with them through the camera lens. It takes a bit of practice. When you look directly into a camera lens, you see a great black hole or sometimes a reversed reflection of yourself. If you are using a teleprompter, you see text scrolling in front of the lens.

To make an effective connection through a camera lens, you have to be able to use the same focused, laser-precision eye contact that you use with individuals, which we described in Chapter 5. Imagine the people who are viewing the tape; they are the individuals you are talking to. Talk to them as you would if they were in the room.

An excellent example of someone who can make very effective eye contact on camera is Bill Clinton. In fact, former President Clinton makes excellent eye contact both live and on camera. Live, he uses the techniques we discussed in Chapter 5, connecting with one person at a time. When his live presentation is being televised, the result is that we viewers at home see someone who is focused and engaged with his audience, even if we can't see the audience. When he makes eye contact directly with the camera lens, he uses that same focus.

Body language on camera

In a live presentation, natural gestures enhance your presentation. But many gestures that are perfectly natural in person seem enormous on camera. (See the enclosed CD-ROM for an example.) If the tape will be later edited (for a newscast, for example), you need to keep all movement to a minimum. If the editor uses a segment of the tape in which you use a sweeping arm gesture, the image may cut to or away from you in the middle of this gesture.

A rule of thumb for gesturing on camera is, use minimal movement unless you need a particular gesture to clarify what you are saying. For example, if you are describing an injury to someone's arm, by all means use a gesture to show how the injury occurred. If you are describing an accident and you can use your hands to explain how each car was traveling and who was cut off by whom, those are good reasons to gesture on camera. If you do use a gesture on camera, make sure you know what the frame is; that is, is it from your waist up or from just below your shoulders? If you are using a gesture to explain information, make sure your hands are on camera. Finally, notice how newscasters use their gestures; they are extremely minimal. This is because they know that wild gestures are not persuasive on camera. They are distracting.

What to wear on camera

Dressing for a camera requires a little extra consideration that is unnecessary when one dresses for a live audience. In addition to all of the do's and don'ts discussed in Chapter 13, one must also consider the following points when assembling a wardrobe for a taped appearance:

1. **Colors.** White causes glare on videotape and creates lighting problems for the videographer. Instead, opt for a light blue shirt. Light colors like sky blue and grey make good choices for shirts. Red and other bright

colors can sometimes "bleed" into the surrounding images on the tape and thus should be avoided. If you know beforehand the color of the backdrop that will be behind you in the taping, avoid wearing that color so you don't blend into the backdrop and look like a floating head on the screen.

2. **Patterns.** Avoid small, busy patterns, like polka dots, checks, and small stripes. These patterns can appear to jump around on videotape.

Epilogue:
We Rest Our Case

There's a fine line between persuasion and manipulation. There are many techniques for persuading others to buy something or to do something. Salesmen, for example, try to create rapport with their clients or ask many questions requiring an affirmative response in order to help create a positive attitude. Some people who attempt to persuade may even tell a little white lie.

An attorney faces numerous situations where he or she needs to persuade. Before a judge or jury, attorneys are charged with persuading the trier of fact of the merits of their case. In depositions, one may want to persuade the person being deposed to open up and trust them. They may consciously use skills such as eye contact, vocal inflection, and body language to achieve this goal.

The challenge is that all of us are conditioned to be wary of "the salesman," the public speaker or presenter, or anyone with an agenda, so we filter the speaker's comments through our personal "lie detectors." We are extremely wary of people who try to persuade us of their point of view. Through radio, television, and the mass media, we are constantly barraged with information and advertising. We have to sift through what is important and what is not. Hence, we are all expert lie detectors in our own minds, and we look for "the pitch." Ultimately, we're afraid of being burned, tricked, or manipulated. This assertion may seem cynical, but we're speaking specifically of the speaker-listener-audience member relationship. Is it possible to persuade without manipulation? The answer is yes, as long as the speaker maintains the appropriate mindset, focus, and attitude.

Usually, when one tries to persuade another, the speaker's mindset is focused on the act of persuasion. As listeners, we have the innate ability to feel the intention, or the mindset, of the person speaking to us. For example, if your doctor is communicating to you the results of a battery of tests, it would become clear to you, the listener, what her mindset is. Is she trying to comfort you? Could be bad news. Is she attempting to warn you? Maybe you have to make some important changes. Is she trying to, perhaps, persuade you of a particular course of treatment? Maybe you should listen with wariness or take it with a grain of salt. In each of these examples, the doctor is pursuing a different goal, so her intention when communicating to you, her patient, is different.

So, as a lawyer conducting an opening statement, what is *your* intention? Are you even aware of your intention? What is your main purpose? Is it to appear relaxed and likeable, or do you want to give the impression of authority?

When speaking to the trier of fact, it is vital that we understand what we are trying to communicate. What is the point of the story that we are telling? What is our intention? Where are we focusing our attention? Is it on ourselves, or on the needs of our listeners?

So many times when we are trying to persuade, our main focus is on ourselves. Things come to mind such as, "I wonder if they notice that my hands are stiff?" or "Shoot, that didn't come out the way that I rehearsed it in my head this morning!" or "The judge isn't looking at me, why isn't she looking at me, did I offend her, she must hate my argument," and so on.

Although this focus and way of thinking is normal for the uninitiated, the next step in the evolution of communication is focusing your attention and your intention on the trier of fact and/or your audience. There are some specific skills that can help us here: effective eye contact, message-enhancing body language, theme and story structure, and vocal skills, just to name a few. All of these different methods of focusing our attention lead us to becoming the most *interested* person in the courtroom, *not* the most *interesting*.

This attitude of interest in the trier of fact is one of the most important factors in effective communication. This is not to be confused with a self-serving interest in being, as Willy Loman says in *Death of a Salesman*, "well liked." The type of interest we're referring to is an *external focus*. Instead of focusing all of our attention on ourselves or even our argument, we instead focus our attitude on building relationships with our audience. Becoming more interested in the people to whom you are speaking is much more interesting and less threatening than trying to overtly "sell" your case.

Of course, when you enter the courtroom, you are prepared. You know what you are trying to accomplish with each sentence uttered. You have rehearsed aloud the key moments in your presentation; for, after all is said and done, after all the motions for summary judgment have been denied and your chances of settlement are slim to none, what you have left is an *oral presentation*. Suddenly, the rules of engagement have completely changed. Now you have to communicate interactively, one human being at a time. This is a person-to-person call.

So are you having a person-to-person call? When you prepare your opening statement, go through the following checklist and ask yourself these questions:

- Do I know exactly what message or theme I am trying to communicate? NOTE: this should be no more than a few sentences.

- What specific gestures can I incorporate to clarify my theme for my listener(s)?

- Am I talking "at" my audience, or am I building relationships with each individual?

By adjusting our mindset from the act of persuasion to the art of communication and purposeful intention, by focusing our attention away from ourselves, and by developing an attitude of becoming the most *interested* person in the courtroom, *not* the most *interesting*, we move away from appearing manipulative (like a salesman) towards the art of communicating person to person, one human being at a time.

We began teaching these skills because we believe strongly that the law is a noble profession. We believe that the justice system in this country works, but only if everyone does their best to make sure that the evidence is clearly presented by the lawyers and understood by the trier of fact. If your argument is clear but the jurors reject it, then maybe your cause was not the right one.

We believe that jurors decide cases based on the evidence, but how they interpret the evidence—what the evidence means to them in the context of your case, what becomes important to them as they make their decisions—depends on how clearly and compellingly you present the evidence.

One of our clients, an excellent trial lawyer in Denver, says, "If they listen to my case and disagree with me, I can live with that. But I just don't want them to walk out of the courtroom and say, 'I just didn't get it.'"

We hope that the skills in this book help you make sure they "get it." We hope that you make your goal of becoming interested in your jurors: in how they need the evidence presented, in what they are hearing and feeling, in how they listen to you. That's how you'll take your skills to the next level. That's how you'll change your practice.

That's how you'll kill *Lawyer Man.*

Contents of the Video CD-ROM

Exercises

Breathing
Breathing Introduction
The Neutral Position
Breathing Exercises

Vocal Skills
Vocal Skills Introduction
Humming
Tongue Twisters

Vocal Inflection
Vocal Inflection Introduction
Your Inflection Sends a
   Message
Controlling the Picture
Identifying Inflections

Body Language
Body Language Introduction
Body Warm-Ups
Gestures to Ehance Your
   Argument
Using the Lectern
Body Language During Video
   Depositions

Eye Contact
Eye Contact Introduction
Where Do You Look?
Take the Time to Look

Worksheets

01 – Vocal Thunder.doc
02 – Body Language.doc
03 – Storytelling.doc
04 – The Credibility Factor.doc
05 – Presence & Spontaneity.doc
06 – Relationships.doc

07 – Witness Preparation.doc
08 – The Deposition You're
       Taking.doc
09 – Eye Contact.doc
10 – Voir Dire.doc
11 – Stage Fright.doc

Instructions for Using the Video CD-ROM

The enclosed *video* CD-ROM contains a series of demonstrations, performed by the authors, of the methods, skills, and exercises discussed in the book. The CD is Windows® 98SE/2000/Me/XP compatible and is playable in your computer's CD-ROM drive. You must have a sound card and speakers connected to your computer in order to hear the audio portion of the CD. *For best results, close all other programs before using this CD.*

The *Winning Edge* program should start automatically when you insert the CD into your computer. If it doesn't, you can run the program manually in one of two ways:

1. Navigate to your CD-ROM drive using Windows Explorer and double-click on the ⬧ WinningEdge.exe file; or

2. Click the **Start** button. Then click **Run...** and type D:\WinningEdge.exe on the "Open" line. Then click the **OK** button to start the program.[2]

The *Winning Edge* program uses *QuickTime 5.0* media player to display the video demonstrations on the CD-ROM. The first time you use the *Winning Edge* program, it will automatically check to see whether you have *QuickTime 5.0* already installed on your computer. If not, the program will automatically install *QuickTime 5.0* for you.

Once the program installs *QuickTime 5.0* and finishes setting itself up, you should see the following full-screen image:

Click the Enter button to begin.

---

[2] NOTE: This assumes your CD-ROM drive is the "D" drive on your computer. If your computer has a different letter designation for your CD-ROM drive, type that letter in place of the D.